First of all, I just have to say this: I love this parenting book! Holy cow! This is stinking amazing. I haven't read too many parenting books because most of them are incredibly unrealistic and eye-rolling cheesy. But this one is excellent. SUPERB. You have so many funny stories (humor is always good) that I have been laughing out loud A LOT. I keep saying to Skip, "Okay you gotta hear this . . . Oh you gotta listen to this . . ." And your insight into those moments is truly wonderful. I just love this book. Overall you have some profound insight, laugh-out-loud moments, and easily applicable concepts. Really good stuff. Your personal stories that you include are appropriate and give such good perspective. I love your transparency.

I like that this is a book about parenting but with a spiritual tone. It's a really good tool for the parent who needs to be equipped.

This is a great start to an excellent book! Another bestseller.

—Carolyn Crust, mother of two

I so appreciate this book; it has been such a wonderful resource to help me put things into check. I feel like we live in such a spoiled, greedy, selfish world and when you stop and think about those around us who are going through so many difficult things, our little things really are little in comparison. I want to teach and show that to my kids. I want them to be more grateful and compassionate. I feel like we have been so negative and judgemental!

And as you put it about the bum on the street, it doesn't mean he's just a lazy drunk, we don't know what happened in his life to put him there but we need to have more compassion for him and take the time to pray for him and those out there who aren't as fortunate as us!

As I look around my house I know my kids have too much. Your book has inspired me to teach my children to give some of it away to someone who doesn't have as much and who could really appreciate it.

I thank you for this book 'cause it has really opened my eyes and my heart and makes me want to do better in the lives of my kids. I want them to grow up grateful and compassionate. I think when this book gets out it will change a lot of lives and hearts!!

This is by far one of the best parenting books I have ever read!!! Thank you so much for letting me be a part of it! You truly have a calling!!

—Kathy Newberg, mother of four

I love the message coming through the pages. Each chapter gives me practical applications, but even more valuable I think is the "concept" teaching you do naturally and with humor and with humility. Thank you. May the Lord continue to strengthen you and give you His message to send out. I can't tell you how many teaching moments are prompted after reading what you wrote ... like the teaching about giving our children a worldview ... so needed. And asking for promised wisdom. As parents we are so easily forget to call on His help and fully engage in His Kingdom work daily. You have a unique way of showing a glimpses of His kingdom work.

—Cindy Larson, mother of two

I LOVE this book! I wish I had it when my kids were young. This book is not only for parents of young children, but for anyone who spends time with children.

—J.T.

As I read the chapters, I sense that God really wants to get across how much He loves us. I don't think women, and most people for that matter, realize just how much God loves them. You mention in chapter 1, "Cultivating a heart of gratitude in our children is impossible unless we ourselves are grateful. We can't impart something we do not posses." This is SO profoundly true. If we don't actually realize God's love for us, how can we be believable when we tell our children this amazing truth? All I have to say is wow and thank you!

I cannot tell you how happy I am that you have written a book like this! Your past struggles are going to help so many people who are in the same place you once were.

—S.J.

As I read this book, I feel like I am getting a "2-for-1" deal! I have read many books on parenting, and this is the first one that does such a great job of helping me to start with me and my life, as it will then spill over into my kids and their lives. I *love* the "Personal Application" followed by the "Parental Application." Such a great re-cap of the chapter with easy, practical ways to use them in our everyday lives. It is humbling and inspiring all at the same time! It feels like I am sharing a cup of tea and encouraging, insightful conversation with you—very relatable. Your humor and candor shine through each chapter. Bless you, for tools and examples from your own personal life that will help me to become a better parent and a better me!

—A.M.

Growing Grateful Kids is such a great source of conviction, encouragement, and inspiration to spur me on to finishing this parenting race well and not sputter out along the way. This book compels me to submit my own character to the refining of the Holy Spirit that I may be equipped to impart those lessons on to my children. Thank you, Susie, for taking the time, for submitting in obedience, and writing this down for a generation in desperate need of this kind of parenting book!

—G.M.

Susie Larson is not just a great author, or great speaker, or great mom; she is a great example of a great example. Her motivation is to tell the world that you too can do anything in partnership with Christ Jesus. She gives us the opportunity to see the weaknesses and successes of her and her family's lives. She is so open with her family examples, because she cares so much about the welfare of other families. I have had the privilege to know Susie for many years. She is what she writes and she has no other agenda than to be doing God's agenda. For anyone who would like the very best for their children or grandchildren, I highly recommend this book—it is a book that will keep on giving, and it will be a legacy to you and yours, inspired by God through Susie.

—L.C., father of four,
and grandfather of 13

Wow. You have put sooooo much good stuff in the book! I am asking God to provide me with the funds to buy a case of books so I can hand them out to every young parent that I know.

—J.T.

This book is an amazing journey to go on with Susie! I love how she bears her heart and experience as a parent throughout it. Each chapter ends with practical ideas for personal and parental application. Be ready to be challenged and transformed by the Holy Spirit in your thinking as you read through this book and apply what you are learning. Your kids will be blessed as you take what you learn and pass it on to them!

—M.N.

In today's society, considerate people are as scarce as rare jewels. In her book *Growing Grateful Kids*, Susie Larson has initiated the process to reverse this socioeconomic calamity. She gives today's mothers the vision of creating a new generation of grateful individuals. She encourages modern mothers, through introspection and changes in their own lives, to teach their children thankfulness in every situation. This book is different from other self-help books because it includes biblically based principles, practical advice, and a keen sense of humor that entice the reader to dig deeper into God's way of *Growing Grateful Kids*.

—P. Larson

Coming from the perspective of a single person with no children, I think this book is an outstanding read! Not only did I gain insight on how to parent from a godly perspective, but I laughed, cried, and was spiritually encouraged to the very last word! I have known the Larsons for several years, so I have seen firsthand what a wonderful example they are for others. I cannot stress enough how important it is for everyone to read this book—it will change your way of thinking on how to parent children in a way that honors God. This is Susie's best book yet!

—S. Johnson

This is the real deal, moms. This book will grab your attention and speak beyond the pages . . . even if you are one of those who has a hard time getting into books. Susie writes with humor, vulnerability, and a depth that calls us to look beyond our own parenting to the example of Jesus. I was SO BLESSED in reading this book and I pray the same be true for you!

—C. Larson

growing grateful kids

TEACHING THEM TO APPRECIATE AN
EXTRAORDINARY GOD IN ORDINARY PLACES

SUSIE LARSON

MOODY PUBLISHERS

CHICAGO

Library of Congress Cataloging-in-Publication Data

Larson, Susie, 1962-
    Growing grateful kids : teaching them to appreciate an extraordinary God in ordinary places / Susie Larson.
        p. cm.
    Includes bibliographical references.
    ISBN 978-0-8024-5282-5
    1. Parenting—Religious aspects—Christianity. 2. Child rearing—Religious aspects—Christianity. 3. Gratitude—Religious aspects—Christianity. I. Title.
BV4529.L274 2010
248.8'45—dc22

2009044343

We hope you enjoy this book from Moody Publishers. Our goal is to provide high-quality, thought-provoking books and products that connect truth to your real needs and challenges. For more information on other books and products written and produced from a biblical perspective, go to www.moodypublishers.com or write to:

Moody Publishers
820 N. LaSalle Boulevard
Chicago, IL 60610

1 3 5 7 9 10 8 6 4 2

Printed in the United States of America

This book is lovingly dedicated to my three sons...

Jake, your compassion and conviction bless me beyond words. May God continue to use you to minister to the least-of-these!

Luke, your integrity and gentleness inspire me greatly. May God continue to use you and your music to usher people into the presence of God!

Jordan, your kindness and humor always make me smile. May God work through you to bring healing to those in need!

And to my husband...

Honey, you are my partner in life. God has moved heaven and earth on our behalf. You are a fabulous father and husband. Bless you for your presence, your gentleness, and your strength. I love you more every day.

And to Jesus...

You show me every day what it means to be Yours. I love You most.

CONTENTS

Section Four: Live Abundantly

FOREWORD

All of us have encountered children who are delightful. Most of us have also seen children who are irritating and some who are downright obnoxious. Why do some children seem happy and content, while others are constantly complaining? Did one get a "happy gene" that the other did not?

We know that children have very different personalities even when they are raised in the same family. Many personality traits have their root in the child's genetic makeup. However, we know that parental influence also plays a major role in the child's attitude and behavior.

Children who are indulged by parents, given whatever they request and allowed to do whatever they desire, are likely to have major problems in establishing healthy adult relationships. The absence of boundaries does not equip children for the real world. These children will become "takers" rather than "givers." Consequently they fail to find the deep satisfaction that comes from genuinely loving others.

Susie Larson believes in the power of parental influence. Not only have she and her husband, Kevin, raised three healthy and responsible sons, she has also learned from thousands and thousands of mothers who have shared their successes and failures on the parental journey.

While she recognizes the important role of fathers, Susie writes primarily to mothers and grandmothers who wish to leave a positive legacy for their children. Single moms will also find this book to be extremely helpful.

What you say and do with your children will greatly influence how they feel about themselves, God, and other people. One of the things I really like about *Growing Grateful Kids* is the emphasis on becoming the kind of person you want your child to be. Your model is your most powerful influence.

What you read in this book may bring tears, will certainly spark smiles, and most importantly will give you ideas that will help you be the responsible mother you desire to be. I predict that you will become a better person and a better parent by reading and applying the principles shared in *Growing Grateful Kids*.

Gary Chapman,
author of *The Five Love Languages* and *Love As a Way of Life*

INTRODUCTION

W*rite a parenting book? Me?*

Can I be honest? I never wanted to write a parenting book. Over the years people asked me to consider the idea, but I always shook my head and said, "I don't want to put my kids out there as examples for the world to look at. They are great guys, but I want to respect their privacy and their growth process. Plus, if I wrote a parenting book, I'd write it from a deeply spiritual perspective—and not so much from an educational standpoint. My idea of a parenting book would be different enough that I would need to know that God is really the one inspiring me to tackle such a project."

God moves us in perfect and timely ways. Almost overnight, my boys turned into men. At the same time, I felt constantly burdened about the state of our young people today. Selfishness and material- ism, a lack of gratitude, respect, and humility are rampant in today's youth. The more I prayed and grieved over this observation, the more clearly the idea for this book took shape in my heart and mind.

Still, I had to consider the matter of my sons' privacy and their own refining processes of growing from boys to men. But when I talked with Jake, Luke, and Jordan about my idea for this book, they didn't blink or pause, they just said, "Do it, Mom. This book needs to be written."

So here I am. Offering you a book that deals with you on two levels—first as a woman, *created in God's image*, and then as a mom (or grandmom), *called by God to raise incredible children.*

You'll notice that I make this statement time and time again throughout the book: "You cannot impart what you do not possess." Our kids need to be grateful, but we cannot teach what we do not know. Therefore, we must become sincerely grateful people first.

Our kids desperately need to know what it means to hear God's voice, but we cannot teach them something we ourselves do not understand. So for our sake and theirs, we must cultivate a lifestyle of listening to God and of doing what He says. Our kids need a living, breathing faith, and they'll see it modeled as we pursue an authentic relationship with Jesus.

Kids today need to care about those who have less than they do. They'll learn compassion by watching us reach out to those in need. So much of parenting comes down to modeling Christ in our everyday lives.

As parents, we need to hit the pause button once in a while and simply play with our children. We'll learn how to enjoy life by watching *them*. When we take time to romp with our kids, we send the world the message that it is God who carries the world on His shoulders, not us.

The journey through this book is twofold; it's for you and for your child. I pray that you will learn things first as a woman, and then, second, as a woman who happens to be a mom. At the end of each chapter you'll notice two points of application: Personal Application and Parental Application. These are simple and practical pieces of advice to help you live out an authentic, grateful life and help you to impart a grateful life to your children as well.

Since my ministry is to women, I wrote this book from one mom to another. You'll notice *only* a handful of references to my husband, but please don't interpret that to mean he was an absent father. Kevin said just the other day, "This book needs to be mom-to-mom because about half of your readers will be single or at least feel like they are." I appreciate his unselfishness in encouraging me to write this book from an up-close-and-personal perspective.

Some of my sample readers are grandparents, and they wanted other grandparents to know that this book is for them too. May you be encouraged to impart faith, humility, and gratitude into the hearts of your grandchildren.

Finally, the question begs to be asked: is it even possible to raise world changers let alone grateful kids in this self-entitled society?

My answer is a resounding YES!

But we need to be the real-deal if we want to give our kids the best chance to rise above the fray and to be everything God intended them to be. Teaching perspective and gratitude to our children in today's world is absolutely critical, but it's not difficult.

Please join me and let's explore the idea that God is a hilarious, wonderful, and present Father. He loves our kids more than we do. You will no doubt laugh at some of our mishaps and crazy stories. But, I pray also that you'll be deeply moved to *know and embrace* your value as a woman and a mother. You are God's precious treasure, and

He has great things for you to do in this life. Raising grateful kids will be one of the most heroic things you will do in your lifetime.

May God richly bless you as you read.

Section One

MODEL THANKFULNESS

be expectant

GOD IS WORKING

And my God will meet all your needs according to his glorious riches in Christ Jesus. **(PHILIPPIANS 4:19)**

"God's gifts put man's best dreams to shame."[1]

—ELIZABETH BARRETT BROWNING

y girlfriends had warned me about the grocery store. And when my girlfriends spoke, I listened. These women were several years ahead of me in the ways of marriage, children, and well, just about everything. Their experience and wisdom always gave me pause and made me consider my steps. One day, my friend said, "If you end up having more than two children, you might not want to attempt to take your little ones with you to buy groceries all by yourself. With treats everywhere in sight and little hands reaching for them, it's stressful to push a bursting shopping cart through the grocery store without losing your mind or possibly losing track of one of your kids."

My hand found its way to my growing belly, and I swallowed

hard. The very thought of taking on such a task seemed more than a little overwhelming since I had yet to give birth to my first child. Though eventually I would have plenty of stressful trips to the store with my three sons, I also remember a time when, for me, it was a different experience altogether.

❁ ❁ ❁

The grocery store was packed with moms and kids. Colorful packages of crackers and cookies promised bursts of flavor. Little toys hung on the endcaps, and children whined while moms pulled their little reaching arms back into the cart.

With my little Jordan in the basket seat and Jake and Luke hanging on to the sides of the cart, I worked up a sweat as I filled my shopping cart with different kinds of food.

After buckling my three little boys into their car seats, I crawled into the driver's seat of my car. It had been a tough few years for us financially. Nearly every dollar that came in went back out the door to pay down our medical debt.

I grabbed the steering wheel and rested my forehead on my hands. I was suddenly awash with gratitude. We had a week's worth of food in the trunk and even a couple of treats for the boys.

"Boys, before we head home, we're going to thank Jesus for all of this food. You know why? Because we have choices about what to eat! Many children won't get even one meal today. We have *several* kinds of cereals and soups. We have sandwiches and crackers. We even have some cookies and juice. Let's say thank You to Jesus."

One by one, the boys folded their hands and bowed their heads. And one by one, we each thanked God for a cart full of food. We were blessed indeed.

❀ ❀ ❀

In the four short years it took me to deliver three babies, we encountered more trials and stresses than I had ever imagined possible. Of course, I was completely naïve and bright-eyed going into marriage and parenting. I watched my friends and decided that my life would be like theirs. They had nice homes, money in the bank, and seemed able to parent out of instinct. I didn't know how or when all of those blessings would arrive for me, but nonetheless, I assumed they'd arrive.

God's blessings did find their way into my life but not in a way that I recognized at first. Our journey turned out to be a different one completely. While my friends took trips, decorated their homes, and bought nice clothes for their children, I spent months lying on my couch—on my left side—trying to prevent premature labor. Our babies struggled with respiratory issues, and I developed a disease that cost us a lot of money to diagnose and to treat.

For us, money was scarce and times were difficult, but one great blessing came in an unlikely package. I didn't want this gift, but God, in His infinite wisdom, blessed us with the gift of our *need*. We needed help.

It's no fun being the desperate one. All of our needs confronted my fear that I would inconvenience others right out of my life. If

I leaned on people too much, they might just go away. If I'm the one with "less-than," then I must *be* "less-than." Yet there I was, in need financially, physically, emotionally, and spiritually. That place of desperation felt like the worst place for me to be. But in fact, it was exactly where I *needed* to be.

I turned to God in prayer. I pondered verses like Philippians 4:19: "And my God will meet all your needs according to his glorious riches . . ." *Really, Lord? Will You really reach into Your abundant supply and share some of it with my family?* I looked out the window and watched the clouds pass overhead. If I believed He was truly busy and active in my life, I had to trust Him to help us in our time of need. And He did.

if I believed He was truly **BUSY AND ACTIVE** in my life, I had to **TRUST HIM** to help us in our time of need.

Somehow, someway, our cereal seemed to last longer than it should. Somehow, someway, I managed to find just the right thing at a garage sale. Out of the blue, a friend would offer me a bag of clothing that her kids had outgrown.

God unexpectedly met our needs in some of the most unlikely ways. At first I wasn't looking for God to show up. I was busy looking at what my friends had and constantly felt great angst that I was one of the have-nots. But when I decided to quit comparing myself with others and to start trusting that God had His own plan for me, my eyes opened to all of the ways God was providing for me, just as He promised.

One night I was covered in suds as I attempted to bathe my three little boys, all at the same time. They giggled and splashed while I soaked up the wet floor with clean towels. My clothes were wet and my bangs were dripping. The doorbell rang, and I was in no shape to answer the door—and I surely wasn't about to leave my three kids in the tub by themselves.

One at a time, I lifted my little guys out of the tub, toweled them off, and helped them put on their pajamas. I actually forgot about the doorbell. Later that night my husband walked into the house carrying a bag of groceries. "You went grocery shopping tonight?" I asked as I greeted him at the top of the stairs. With a half smile, he said, "No, this bag was sitting on our doorstep. No note, just the food."

I brushed my wet bangs out of my eyes and thought back to the ringing doorbell. I imagined someone standing on our doorstep with food. I felt bad that I didn't even get to the door to thank the kind person who delivered such a timely gift. Even so, their sweet gift made me feel loved and cared for.

Though our struggles were real, God's love was more real still. And we were beginning to see Him everywhere in ways big and small.

The Lord was my provider and my refiner. He promised to supply all of my needs but He wanted me looking at *Him* (not at my friends' possessions). This is not to say that my friends never struggled or fought their own battles. They did. This is also not to say that I walked gracefully and embraced trust during our most trying times, because, to be quite frank, sometimes I kicked and screamed and threw my pillow across the bedroom in frustration and cried, "How long until You rescue us, Lord? How long until things don't feel so difficult?" I'd pray and cry and wait silently in God's presence, and every time His words would come back to me: *I will supply all of your needs, according to My riches, not yours.*

I didn't always want to hear those words. I wanted my way. But during the times when I was actually willing to lay down my agenda and pick up God's promise to provide, I found a peace that was better than getting my way. I found something else too—the desire to thank Jesus for what I already had.

One morning I awoke to the task of making breakfast for my three little ones. I looked in the cupboard and already knew what I'd find. No cereal. No oatmeal. Just an almost-empty box of pancake mix sat on the shelf. Surely the neighbors would loan me some cereal if I asked them, but I couldn't bring myself to ask them. People had already helped us on numerous occasions. I was tired of being the friend who was always in need. Besides, we had pancake mix.

Something fluttered in my stomach at the thought of making this a special morning in spite of our desperate financial situation. With my three little boys seated in their booster chairs around the table, I eagerly set down one big plate before them, and four forks. Before our eyes sat one large pancake with a single flickering candle standing up in the middle.

Sitting on my knees on my chair so I could lean in especially close, I asked the boys to fold their hands and then I continued, "Guys, aren't we just so blessed today? The sun is shining. We have each other. Daddy's out there working hard for us. And God provided this big giant pancake for us to have for breakfast! Let's thank Him for taking such good care of us."

Enjoying our little celebration and without skipping a beat, the boys leaned in, bowed their heads, and in their own way, thanked

Jesus for our wonderful breakfast. They were giddy at the thought of an unexpected celebration. Afterwards we went outside and played together in the sandbox. That breakfast with my boys filled me with joy and taught me much about choosing a right perspective. As far as my boys were concerned, they had everything they needed. As far as I was concerned—at least at that moment—I did too.

It's a good thing to have all the props pulled out from under us occasionally. It gives us some sense of what is rock under our feet, and what is sand.[2] — Madeleine L'Engle

The disciples were exhausted. They had worked nonstop all day ministering to the needs of the people. *So many families.* So few disciples. Thousands of men, women, and children crowded together on the hillside, all with needs, all waiting to see Jesus. Antsy children ran amidst the throngs of people. Jesus and His disciples prayed for and ministered to the sick and the suffering *all day long.* Imagine a mother handing her desperately ill daughter to Jesus. Imagine Jesus handing back to the mother a perfectly healthy, wonderfully healed little girl. Picture it.

The day turned into evening. Fatigue set in. Possibly fifteen thousand people (the Bible tells us five thousand *besides* women and children) had gathered that day for a touch from Jesus. And hours later, the multitudes remained. Imagine the various groups of men standing together and talking about the day. Imagine little children leaning into the arms of their moms and whining about their growling stomachs. Envision this scene.

As evening approached, the disciples came to [Jesus] and said, "This is a remote place, and it's already getting late. Send the crowds away, so they can go to the villages and buy themselves some food." (Matthew 14:15)

Every mother, at some point or another, feels overwhelmed, outnumbered, and insufficient to meet the needs before her. In ourselves, we *aren't* enough for the lofty task of motherhood. Jesus understands our predicaments. His disciples faced impossible situations regularly. But it's in our places of desperate need that Jesus makes Himself known.

When our strength is unequal to the task, we see the strength of God come to bear in our lives. And when what we hold in our hand falls short of the need before us, we can keep perspective because we have a place to go with our need. We have a God who makes up where we lack. We have an engaged Father who lovingly provides for us. We have reason to be thankful.

Let's take a look at Jesus' response to what would be an impossible predicament for us; but first, let's remember again the scenario. Possibly fifteen thousand people were under the care of thirteen men (the disciples and Jesus). They hadn't eaten in hours, and it's

> it's in our places
> of **DESPERATE NEED**
> that Jesus makes
> Himself **KNOWN**.

likely that at least a few people and children were feeling a tad bit irritable. The disciples were ready for a break. They had, after all, been on duty all day. And they didn't, after all, have a budget to feed thousands of people. So you can understand why they asked Jesus to tell the people to go away and find some food for themselves.

Jesus replied, "They do not need to go away. You give them something to eat." "We have here only five loaves of bread and two fish," they answered. "Bring them here to me," he said. And he directed the people to sit down on the grass. Taking the five loaves and the two fish and looking up to heaven, he gave thanks and broke the loaves. Then he gave them to the disciples, and the disciples gave them to the people. (Matthew 14:16–19)

First, Jesus acknowledged what He had: five loaves and two fish. Not a bad meal for a small handful of people—but for thousands and thousands? Jesus took what He had, and He looked up to heaven. *He gave thanks.* And then He gave the food to the disciples who in turn fed the people.

They all ate and were satisfied, and the disciples picked up twelve basketfuls of broken pieces that were left over. The number of those who ate was about five thousand men, besides women and children. (Matthew 14:20–21)

They all ate. They all were satisfied. And there were *leftovers.* What a miracle! How do we follow Jesus' example? We take our little offerings, we look up to heaven, we thank God for His faithfulness, and then we go about our day. That's the stuff of miracles.

Cultivating a heart of gratitude in our children is impossible unless we ourselves are grateful. We can't impart something we do not possess. Always as moms, first and foremost, we have to keep a close watch on our own attitude, which is fueled by our perspective.

In good seasons and in difficult ones, we are under God's care, and He has *promised* to meet our needs. Therefore, we are called to give thanks.

Give thanks in all circumstances; for this is the will of God in Christ Jesus for you. (1 Thessalonians 5:18 ESV)

Sometimes giving thanks will feel like a "sacrifice of praise" because it will cost us something. This is not to say that we thank God *for* the painful things we endure, but rather, we thank Him amidst those difficult times. We thank Him *in* the pain, not for it. Just what does that look like on a practical level? Something like this:

Dear Father,

These are desperate times for us, and we are tempted to fear, but we know that You are faithful. You are faithful! Give us a bigger perspective during this trial. Remind us again that You know our need. We praise You ahead of time for the mighty ways You will come through for us. Open our eyes so we can see You in the many surprising ways You plan on showing up along the way. Amen.

Dear friend, know that those kinds of prayers are a fragrant offering to your heavenly Father. It's a very big deal to God when His people pray in faith though they have lots of reasons to fear.

At times it will be *easier* to fret, complain, and to voice our fears in front of our children. Life gets stressful and countless things can shake our confidence and our footing. This is where our faith really counts. This is where our children have the potential of learning great things from us.

"Do you see what we've got? An unshakable kingdom! And do you see how thankful we must be? Not only thankful, but brimming with worship, deeply reverent before God. For God is not an indifferent bystander" (Hebrews 12:28, THE MESSAGE).

Some days you'll need a loaves and fishes miracle, other days it will be enough to see a flower in the crack of the sidewalk. Nothing is too difficult for Him. Not that He's bound to satisfy our every whim, but He has made a mighty promise to us: to supply all of our needs and to fulfill the desires of our heart— when we find our delight in Him.

> some days you'll need a **LOAVES AND FISHES** miracle, other days it will be enough to see a **FLOWER** in the crack of the **SIDEWALK.**

Also, your children will pick up on your perspective. When you truly look for God's promises to come to bear in the day-to-day life as a wife, a mother, and a woman, *you* will find Him faithful. And when you model a heart of gratitude—even during sparse seasons—your children will feel settled, secure, and cared for.

personal application:

• The minute your feet hit the floor in the morning, say out loud for your own ears to hear, "Every day I'm in God's presence, and He will provide for me!"

• Spend time with God each day. Lots of time. As much time as you are able. Meditate on verses that talk about being thankful. Prayerfully thank God for His faithfulness. Believe it or not, this will build your faith!

• Start a thankfulness journal. Whenever you're feeling blue, take some time and write down EVERY thing for which you're thankful, e.g., clean, running water, a roof over your head, your husband, children, friends, church, and so on.

parental application:

• Each day, allow your children to hear you making "thankful" statements, e.g., "Look at the beautiful sky God painted for us today!" "Aren't these sandwiches great?" "I'm so glad to be your mom." "I'm thankful God made you so kind."

• During trying times, find the blessing in them, e.g., When you come out of the doctor's office, buckle your kids in and together pray something like, "God, we thank You that we have a doctor to go to when we're sick. We pray for all of the sick children who can't afford a doctor. Bless them too."

- At meal times, pick a child to pray for the meal and ask her to say what she's thankful for.
- Go around the table at dinner times and share highlights and low-lights about the day. Celebrate the highlights and help the children find perspective regarding the lowlights.

Dear Lord,

Help me to remember that You are always good, You're always work-ing, and You're always thinking of me. Forgive me for my tendency to grumble, complain, and worry. Everywhere I look I see evidences of Your mercy and kindness. Thank You for my home, for running water, for clothes to wear, and for freedom. Remind me to practice gratitude every single day. Help me to voice my blessings far more than my burdens. You are always up to something. Help me to cultivate expectant faith in my home. May my children continually grow in the knowledge that You are good. Amen.

refuse worry

GOD IS FAITHFUL

Do not be anxious about anything, but in everything by prayer and supplication with thanksgiving let your requests be made known to God. **(PHILIPPIANS 4:6 ESV)**

✦ "Worry is an indication that we think God cannot look after us."[1] ✦

—*OSWALD CHAMBERS*

ssurance grows in unexpected places. I remember a particular summer day many years ago when a single flower poking up through the ground brought me to my knees and moved me to tears. We were in the midst of one painful season after another. Apparently several spring and summer seasons had come and gone without much notice from me. For many years in a row, life felt like a cold, dreary winter. It honestly hadn't even occurred to me that my favorite seasons had come and gone without my noticing them.

There, in that place, life continued to be hard. I was still battling a disease while trying to parent three very young and extremely active boys. My energy was still low and my faith still wavered from time to time.

Even money was still scarce, but, like Jack and the Beanstalk, I had some seeds. Mine came in the mail. Maybe they were part of a garden-ing promotion or maybe it was a neighbor's anonymous attempt to help me put some color in my life. I don't know. What I did know was that it was springtime and I had some seeds in my hand.

I rounded up my little guys and showed them the beautiful pic-ture on the front of the packet. Then I opened it up and showed them the ugly little seeds inside. Luke wrinkled his nose and said, "Somebody's not telling the truth. Those aren't flowers." I chuckled and then explained the wonder of life in a seed.

The boys and I padded out to the backyard and found a patch of dirt right next to our concrete patio. With six dirty little hands helping me to clear a spot for our seeds, we were ready in no time. I planted the seeds, and we watered them. Then life got hard again, and I forgot all about my little investment.

Our medical debt weighed like a big heavy boulder on my back. My uncontrollable and unpredictable disease left me feeling as vul-nerable as a woman living in a run-down part of town with no locks on her doors. Seeing the weariness on my friends' faces (from help-ing me) made me wonder when they would wise up and find a new friend. Everywhere I turned I found reasons to worry.

Did it really matter that I was a Christian? Did it matter whether I prayed or not? Could it be true that a small seed of faith is enough to move a mountain? The Bible says it's true. But when I looked at the piles of problems in my life and looked at the promises from

Scripture, I was tempted to do what Luke did: wrinkle my nose and say, "Somebody's not telling the truth." And the thing was, somebody *was* lying to me, but it wasn't God.

I never let myself stay in those doubtful places for very long because I knew in my heart of hearts that God was the strength of my heart and my portion forever.

Yet I am always with you; you hold me by my right hand. You guide me with your counsel, and afterward you will take me into glory. Whom have I in heaven but you? And earth has nothing I desire besides you. My flesh and my heart may fail, but God is the strength of my heart and my portion forever. (Psalm 73:23–26)

Even though doubt was not a regular struggle for me, I did wander over to the ways of worry with great regularity.

What if we lose our house? What if one of my children gets sick and dies? What if this disease spins out of control and *I* die? I couldn't bear the thought of missing out on raising my precious, treasured heirs. The giants in my land had loud voices and each swung a big stick. I was no match for them.

But then again, David was no match for Goliath either. Goliath outsized and outweighed David. He yelled loud and was just plain mean. He spouted personal insults at David and laughed in his face. Does that sound like someone you know? Hint: he's mean, ugly, and cartoons paint him red and put a pitchfork in his hand.

Without the Lord at our side, we are no match for the enemy. The devil is loud and knows how to exaggerate our problems.

But then there's God. He uses our everyday circumstances and resources to teach us truth and to show us His faithfulness. He uses seeds, slings, stones, and whatever else we have in our midst. Then He teaches us how to take out the giants in our land.

David took out this loud obnoxious giant with a sling and a stone, the very things God had equipped him to use during his years as a shepherd boy. David could have worried and cowered before his mighty opponent. But instead, he said yes to God and he moved forward in faith. In fact, he did more than that. When Goliath hurled his insults and threats at David, David yelled back a declaration of the faithfulness of almighty God!

Then David said to the Philistine, "You come to me with a sword and with a spear and with a javelin, but I come to you in the name of the Lord of hosts, the God of the armies of Israel, whom you have defied. This day the Lord will deliver you into my hand . . . that all the earth may know that there is a God in Israel, and that all this assembly may know that the Lord saves not with sword and spear. For the battle is the Lord's, and he will give you into our hand."

(1 Samuel 17:45–47 ESV)

❀ ❀ ❀

I've known many women (and I was one myself) who, though they loved Jesus and considered themselves *believers*, regularly voiced their fears and worries in front of their children. We wouldn't feed our kids poison for lunch, and yet we think nothing of spouting off all of the reasons we are stressed, worried, and afraid of the giants in our land. If our default response is to declare defeat in the face of our foes, then our children will assume that it pays more to worry than it does to wait on God. Their roots will be shallow at best because ours are too.

We plant seeds with every word we say. The thing is . . . are we planting weeds or something beautiful? Do our own words weaken our outlook (and that of our children's) or do they impart faith and perspective? When we bump up against difficult people, do our children learn love and humility by what we say? Or do they learn how to be two people; either to be calm to save face, or to spout when they think no one is listening?

It is tough to teach our children to "be kind" if we are mean and petty. We'll have a difficult time encouraging them to "trust Jesus" if we cling to fear and make provisions for plans B, C, and D. At some point we have to become more like Jesus—which takes humility and a teachable spirit. Also, at some point, we have to shift the weight of our cares onto the faithfulness of God—so much so that if He doesn't come through for us, we are sunk without Him. That kind of faith pleases God and is so authentic that it leaves a remarkable impression on our children.

Not that we're always going to do this right. We will all choose fear over faith on occasion, and we will each do our share of spouting, pouting, and venting when our lives overheat. We are absolutely going to

> we plant **SEEDS**
> with every word
> we say. The thing
> is . . . are we
> planting **WEEDS**
> or something
> **BEAUTIFUL?**

blow it from time to time. We're going to yell, scream, clench our fists, and stomp our feet. There will be days when our hissy fits make us look like two-year-olds dressed up in a grown-up's body. It's important to note that *Jesus loves us even on those days*. He knows how difficult it can be to parent little ones. Even so, when our kids see us blowing a gasket, they also need to see what the restoration process looks like.

We need to walk our children before the Lord, let them see us asking for forgiveness and a renewed perspective. We need to paint our kids a picture of what the higher road looks like—even though we ourselves stumble along the low road on occasion—and we must use our own missteps and mistakes as opportunities to teach them the blessings of repentance and forgiveness.

Life gets stressful, and we are perfectly human. But God has made a way for us, right here, right now. We cannot get away from His love, and every situation is an opportunity to learn more about His faithfulness.

Regardless of the stress of our circumstances, this one thing is still true: worry looks at life without God in mind. Every single time I got tangled up in worry it was because I had lost my perspective. Like those rope traps that circle your feet and turn you upside down, I had lost my footing, and thus, my frame of reference.

And yet Jesus tells us, "Do *not* worry." Don't do it. Don't go there. Walk away from worry. Have no part of it. Don't worry about *any-thing*. Instead, pray about *everything*. Tell God what you need and *don't forget* to thank Him *when* He answers.

Give your entire attention to what God is doing right now, and don't get worked up about what may or may not happen tomorrow. God will help you deal with whatever hard things come up when the time comes. (Matthew 6:34 THE MESSAGE)

Jesus gives us a clear directive here, which implies that we have some choice in the matter. We are the bosses of our perspectives. We make the choice to entertain worry or to walk away from it. In my early years of parenting, I really didn't fully understand this truth. Nor did I truly understand the impact of my perspective on my children's lives.

My three boys had just finished breakfast and were ready to go outside to play in the sandbox. Everything was an effort for me, but I decided the fresh air would be good for all of us. We opened the sliding door and walked outside. Instantly one of the boys yelled, "Momma! Look!" Luke's little chubby hand pointed to the dirt pile where we had planted seeds about a month ago. There amidst our makeshift garden stood one single flower. A healthy, beautiful flower.

I was instantly overcome. I plopped to my knees on the grass and put my face in my hands. And I wept. *Seasons do change. Through my tears, I said to myself, It isn't winter anymore. I can say for sure that it's summertime. The sun is shining, and though I don't feel all that great, I'm here with my kids, staring at a miracle—proof that it matters if I plant seeds or I don't.*

That flower was the most beautiful thing I'd ever seen. How is it that an ugly little seed could produce such a beautiful work of art? I couldn't get my mind around it all. But I knew that God was speaking to me.

> how is it that an **UGLY LITTLE SEED** could produce such a **BEAUTIFUL** work of art?

After I planted those seeds, I barely thought of them again. But seeds hold in them the promise of life. Of course, seeds do better if you care for and nurture them. But how sweet of God to allow me this picture of His grace and mercy. How many prayers had I prayed that God had answered and yet I neglected to thank Him? How many seeds of faith had I planted and then just walked away, while God still tended to them?

Even when we're faithless, God is still faithful.

❀ ❀ ❀

God's promises are almost always linked with our obedience. When we love Him and trust Him enough to do what He asks of us, we can know that we are in the center of His will, and that He will provide for us, He will preserve us in battle, and He will not allow the giants in our land to overtake us. Read the Scriptures; over and over again you'll see how deeply God's heart is engaged with those whose hearts are fully devoted to Him, to those who tend to the things that He cares about.

If the Lord delights in a man's way, he makes his steps firm; though he stumble, he will not fall, for the Lord upholds him with his hand. I was young and now I am old, yet I have never seen the righteous forsaken or their children begging bread. They are always generous and lend freely; their children will be blessed.
(Psalm 37:23–26)

Do you struggle with and worry about perpetual financial heartache? First, let me ask you a bold question. Are you currently tithing? Are you—whenever possible—giving to the poor and to those who have less than you? Too often we wonder why God allows us to struggle when our very struggle is linked with our disregard of God's commands for our lives. I know it's difficult to take an inventory like this one, but in order to activate the promises of God in our lives, we must first activate obedience to God in our lives.

Okay, so say that you are doing the things God is asking of you and you're still struggling financially. This is where you stand in faith and say out loud, loud enough for your children to hear you: "Our God will come through for us! He is faithful, and He will not forsake us! We will not be moved!"

Like young David against Goliath, this is where we raise the battle cry and proclaim: "Here is yet another opportunity for us to see what an extraordinary God we serve! He will fight this battle for us. And we will stand in faith!" In due time, I promise you, your breakthrough will come.

When I finally got a hold of this concept of declaring victory in the face of worry, circumstances began to change all around me.

Crazy as it sounds I literally marched around inside my house and spoke *life* into my circumstances. I held my checkbook up in the air and declared, "My God will supply all of our needs according to His riches . . . not mine!" I placed my hand on the heads of my three little boys and boldly said, "You three young men are going to be mighty in God! Full of faith and conviction! You are going to do great things for Jesus!" I didn't stop there. I had more victories to claim. I reached my arms in the air and said out loud, "I will not die but live, and declare the works of the Lord! I am strong and healthy, and I will live out the number of my days in health."

Now, lest you think I had temporarily lost my mind, think again. The Bible says that faith comes from *hearing* the Word of God. When my own ears heard my own mouth declare the faithfulness of God, worry scurried away like a little rat that just spotted a giant trap, and my soul was strengthened in the process. Furthermore, as I spoke life and bold faith into my kids, they reflected it back to me when I least expected it.

When I was weary, worn out, or afraid, their little voices spoke volumes to me. Just when I needed my own dose of faith, my sons said things like, "Momma, God is with us; it's going to be okay." Or "Momma, Jesus is working even if we can't see Him." Or "Momma, let's pray right now. And then can I have a cookie?" Sometimes the bigness of their faith confronted the smallness of mine. Still, I learned that every seed planted in the soil of

> when my own ears heard my own mouth declare the **FAITHFULNESS** of God, worry **SCURRIED** away like a little rat that just spotted a giant trap.

their fertile souls produced life and strength and stability.

One of the reasons I wanted to write this book for moms of younger children is because if you cultivate an active faith culture in your home when your children are young, it will be all they know. Not that it's too late to march around your house making bold statements of faith when your kids are in their teens, but it will be so foreign to them that they may not know what to make of it all.

My sons are grown now, and we have lots of conversations about those wilderness years. Their perspectives amaze me. Though they know that their younger years were marked by crisis, they don't remember life being difficult, or scary, or even unstable. Jake said it best: "I know we went through some pretty difficult seasons because you told me so. But I don't really remember life being tough for us. When I think of those years, I remember a loving home where faith was constantly talked about and where Jesus was very real. I had a great home life."

Consequently, faith comes from hearing the message, and the message is heard through the word of Christ. (Romans 10:17)

Maybe you worry about raising your children in this secular society. Totally understandable. What's the best thing you can do for them? Be serious about your own relationship with Jesus. *You love them best when you love Him most.* He is the source of life in every way. The more connected you are to Him, the more assured you'll be of His faithfulness to your children.

Praise the Lord. Blessed is the man who fears the Lord, who finds great delight in his commands. His children will be mighty in the land; the generation of the upright will be blessed. Wealth and riches are in his house, and his righteousness endures forever. Even in darkness light dawns for the upright, for the gracious and compassionate and righteous man. Good will come to him who is generous and lends freely, who conducts his affairs with justice. Surely he will never be shaken; a righteous man will be remembered forever. He will have no fear of bad news; his heart is steadfast, trusting in the Lord. His heart is secure, he will have no fear; in the end he will look in triumph on his foes. He has scattered abroad his gifts to the poor, his righteousness endures forever; his horn will be lifted high in honor. (Psalm 112:1–9)

One thing I learned about worry is this: you can walk away from it. Turn your back on it. Refuse to entertain it. Be free from it. Okay, that's several things, but you get the point. One of the greatest gifts you can give to your children is the gift of assurance, modeled by a heart at peace. Not that you pretend everything is always okay when it isn't. But amidst your heartache and struggle, you can kneel down to your children's level, look in their eyes, pull them close, and let them hear you say, "One thing I know. God will not forsake us." This is a priceless gift for which your children will one day thank you.

What we sow, we grow. Plant seeds of gratefulness right in the middle of your wilderness seasons. Refuse worry and embrace faith every chance you get. Purposely instill thoughts of faith and perspective into your children. Live close to the heartbeat of Christ. Model a humble, thankful heart. Refuse to give your children everything they want, but assure them God will provide everything they need. Take God's offer of peace in every single season.

personal application:

• As soon as worry creeps up, identify it, find its source (is it money, friends, marriage, kids?), and bring it to God. Refuse to entertain anxious thoughts. Apply the verse at the beginning of this chapter (Philippians 4:6).

• Practice gratitude out loud every day. There are thousands of things to be thankful for. Find them and express your thankfulness to God.

• Memorize a few Bible verses that speak to your specific area of worry. Pray them every day.

• Get some exercise. This will do wonders for your mental, physical, and spiritual health.

parental application:

• Teach your children to pray by praying with them. Teach them how to thank God for the blessings in their lives.

• When your children get stressed and worried, sit down with them and walk them all the way through their scenario. Teach them how fear and worry can lie to them. Help them understand God's faithfulness.

• If your child is going through an extended trial that is causing them to worry, make sure you are especially engaged with them during this time. Talk often; pray even more; help them sort through their feelings.

Faithful Lord,

Forgive me for the ways that I am prone to worry. I'm so forgetful! I forget that You are always good and totally faithful. Lead me in Your everlasting way. If my worry is a result of my own disobedience, show me how to make it right. Help me to live in the center of Your will. Help me to cultivate peace and rest in the home. I trust in You and I will not be afraid. Thank You, Lord. Amen.

practice restraint

GOD WILL PROVIDE

And my God will supply every need of yours according to his riches in glory in Christ Jesus. (**PHILIPPIANS 4:19 ESV**)

> "If a child sees his parents day in and day out living without self-restraint or self-discipline, then he will come in the deepest fibers of his being to believe that that is the way to live."[1]
>
> — *M. SCOTT PECK*

grew up in a large family. On the outside, we looked like your basic middle-class family with too many mouths to feed. On the inside, we were a horde of siblings each strategizing to survive until the next time our mom went grocery shopping. Yes, we loved each other, but that love was sometimes upstaged by our greater love for food.

I remember one time looking through my little sister's dresser drawer for a shirt I had loaned her. I didn't find my shirt but I did find a nice stash of snacks she had stolen from the cupboard. Greedy little varmint. I looked both ways, stuffed a couple of treats in my pocket and slipped out of her room. I guess I had a little bit of that greed running through my veins as well.

Growing up in a family with seven kids was a wild ride. We definitely got our exercise. Sometimes we chased each other around the house for the last Ho-Ho or for a measly bite of an Oreo cookie. I'm not sure why those treats had such a stranglehold on us, but they did. Treat battles are not completely without merit, though. I learned one of life's greatest lessons from an encounter with my brother's Twinkie.

One day while minding my own business sitting at the kitchen table drawing in a notebook, my brother Jeff sat down across from me with a Twinkie in his hand. Instantly I dropped my pen, licked my chops, and gazed lustfully at that yellow treat. Without taking my eyes off of the Twinkie, I asked my brother, "Where'd you get it? Twinkies have been gone for four days now."

Realizing his newfound power over me, Jeff slowly turned the Twinkie in his hand, eyeing it from every angle. He took one bite and savored the Twinkie like it was his first bite of food after awaking from a seven-year coma. I licked my lips and imagined the taste of that Twinkie in my mouth. I looked up at Jeff and said, "Can . . . I have it?"

To my surprise, Jeff said, "Sure." Actually, I never did hear him say those words because the moment he opened his mouth to speak, I reached across the table to grab the yellow treasure out of his hands. The problem was, while I thrust my hand toward him, he reached toward me and our hands collided. That glorious whipped lard and sugar filling squished all over my hand. I ruined the Twinkie. Worse than my Twinkie accident was my brother's sweet response: "Susie, I really *was* going to give it to you. I have another one in my drawer."

I was so intent on getting my way that I never thought for a moment that my brother would willingly share his treasure with me.

Skip ahead a number of years. Several times throughout my adult years, I've been tempted to grab for myself something that God had intended on providing for me. Each and every time I heard God's gentle whisper in my heart, "You're about to grab the Twinkie again. Don't do it. Trust Me instead."

Silly as it sounds, this worked for me because I remembered the insatiable craving that compelled me to grab for myself. And, as clear as day, I remember thinking how much sweeter it would have been to be on the receiving end of a generous gift, rather than holding a mashed-up, "less-than" version of what the giver had in mind for me.

Every time I refused to grab something for myself and instead waited before the Lord with open hands, Jesus surprised me anew with His generosity and willingness to share His treasures with me.

❁ ❁ ❁

But I say, walk by the Spirit, and you will not gratify the desires of the flesh. (Galatians 5:16 ESV)

In this day of entitlement, self-restraint has become a lost art. Or better said, a lost fruit, since it is a fruit of the Spirit. We do ourselves (and our kids) a great disservice if we never practice restraint. Just because we can afford something, doesn't mean we should buy it. Just because we have the food in the fridge, doesn't mean we should eat it. Just because it's on TV, doesn't mean we should watch it. On a regular basis, every week, I think, we should say no to ourselves, and then make ourselves deal with it.

Because of my significant health struggles, I was never able to fast for more than a day. I needed my consistent nourishment or else my health diminished. However, I was intent on experiencing the blessing of self-restraint, so I often practiced partial fasts. I fasted from certain meals, kinds of food, TV, the phone, novels (I love my Christian novels so this was a sacrifice for me), and so on. I used that time to more earnestly seek after God. I likened the hunger in my belly to the hunger in my heart.

One of the biggest reasons I practiced fasting was because I wanted nothing to master me. Whenever I settled into a regular indulgence to the point of needing to have "it" to be happy, I knew it was time to go without that particular thing. I just hated the thought of having such little restraint that I was compelled to serve my "thing" rather than have it serve me.

As soon as I noticed myself developing an addictive attachment to something that wasn't necessarily sinful in itself (but required selfishness on my part to accommodate it), I knew it was time to lay it down for a while. Not for legalism's sake, but for freedom's sake.

For different periods of time I laid down things like my flavored coffee, eating at night, TV and movies, a frozen yogurt treat with a bunch of great toppings (that was back when I could eat dairy), and party foods (chips, popcorn, treats). To me, practicing restraint was like exercising a muscle. The more often I said no to myself, the easier it was to do so when it really mattered.

But I discipline my body and keep it under control, lest after preaching to others I myself should be disqualified. (1 Corinthians 9:27 ESV)

> the more often I said **NO TO MYSELF,** the **EASIER** it was to do so when it really **MATTERED.**

We cannot out-give God. When we lay something down for the greater purpose of knowing Him and becoming more like Him, we always come out ahead. Every time I fasted, God blessed me with a newfound perspective and an increased strength mentally, physically, and spiritually.

I decided to try it out on my kids. Every once in a while I'd notice that a certain toy, video game, or movie had attached itself to one of my son's lives in such a way that it was hard to tell where one ended and the other began. As far as my sons were concerned, they *had* to have that thing to be okay. Thankfully for them, I knew they would be okay without it, and I would prove it to them.

By the way, it's important to note that *fasting* from a toy or a movie was not considered a punishment but rather an opportunity for my boys to grow in health and gratitude. Albeit, I did take away toys as a form of discipline on occasion, but I made sure they understood the distinction between the two.

Whenever I sensed it was time for a fast, I'd say something like this, "I think it's time to fast from your video game for a while." After gasping for air they'd ask, "What? Huh? No! I love it! I have to have it! Pleeeeeease, Mom!" I'd reply, "Honey, you are stronger than you think. And though you think you can't live without this game, *you can*. And I'll prove it to you. Besides, nothing on earth should have this kind of power over you. We serve God, not these goofy toys. Let me have it, please."

It was hard to watch them go through toy withdrawal for the first couple of days. But then they got over it and found something else to do. It's an amazing phenomenon, really. Once you get past the pain of self-denial, there's actually relief on the other side. My boys always found in short order that they didn't need any toy to be okay. And when they finally did get their toy back, something beautiful happened. My boys were grateful.

Imagine, an old toy inspiring fresh gratitude. But even more important, that lying stranglehold of "I can't live without this, and I'll die if I don't have it" was broken. My boys never once returned to their unhealthy affections for a toy once they realized they could live without it.

Several years ago while working on an article deadline, my computer froze up. Minutes later Luke poked his head in my office to ask me a question. Being the computer geek that he is, I was excited to have him get my computer working again. "Honey," I asked, "can you please help me with my computer? I'm on a deadline and I need this thing to work for me."

Luke tilted his head, gave me a halfway smile, and said, "Oh, Mom, I wish I could. But I've been fasting from computers for the last month. I decided they were getting too important to me." Then he perked up and said, "But I can help you on Wednesday."

A man without self-control is like a city broken into and left without walls. (Proverbs 25:28 ESV)

If we lack self-control, we leave ourselves (and our kids) wide open to the influences of our culture. Our "no" will be nonexistent or weak at best if we never take it out and use it on ourselves. When tempted to buy something we can't afford, all of our justifications will resound louder than our "no." When our kids plead and beg for something we've already told them they cannot have (and for good reason), their loud whining will wear us down, and we'll end up feeding their sense of entitlement.

In biblical times, the wall that surrounded a city was its protection from enemies who wanted to break in and destroy the safety and freedom of the townspeople. If a life without self-control is like a city with broken-down walls, just how protected are we from the schemes of the enemy?

Now is a good time to take inventory of the "wall" that surrounds us. Do we have a good, healthy "NO" within us? Is our protective fortress strong? When our children are with their friends or at a home with a slightly different standard, do they have it in them to say "NO" if necessary?

Though we wanted our boys to have both Christian and non-Christian friends, we did say this to them: "You can't hang around anybody you can't stand up to. If their opinion matters more than your conviction,

> if a life without **SELF-CONTROL** is like a city with **BROKEN-DOWN WALLS,** just how protected are we from the schemes of the **ENEMY?**

you're not strong enough to walk with them."

Right now, at this time in your life, how able are you to exercise self-control? Do you view it as a great opportunity to grow strong in faith and deep in gratitude? While under your roof, are your children learning that it's not good for them to get everything they want? In fact, are they learning how much better it is for them that they don't?

It is better to be patient than powerful; it is better to have self-control than to conquer a city. (Proverbs 16:32 NLT)

❁ ❁ ❁

One day while sitting at the airport gate waiting for a flight out to a speaking engagement, I met a woman named Sandra. She was a retired high school teacher. We struck up a conversation about raising grateful kids in this materialistic, self-entitled world. She talked about her experiences with selfish, spoiled kids whose parents constantly catered to their every whim and who regularly bailed their children out of trouble. She expressed her frustration at their lack of character (both the kids and their parents) and grieved over all of the missed opportunities to teach these kids about honor, dignity, and respect. Then she said something I'll not soon forget (my paraphrase):

In my thirty plus years of teaching, I've come to realize that many times neglected kids actually turn out better in the long run, than do the overindulged, spoiled kids who get everything they want in life. Neglected kids don't assume that the world revolves around them, and, when they receive something, they're usually thankful for it. On the other hand, I've found that the overindulged, entitled kids possess the same characteristics as the drug addicted students I worked with. Both exuded entitlement, felt the rules didn't apply to them, were selfish, made excuses, and couldn't do much for themselves. They were weak in relationships, weak in employment, and rather than contributing to their surroundings, they drained it of its resources.

God have mercy on us. When we oversaturate our kids with the latest and greatest trinkets and toys, *we actually ruin our children.* When we bail our kids out so they don't have to struggle, *we actually weaken them.* When we make excuses for our kids so that they don't have to feel bad about their behavior, *we deceive them into thinking they don't need a Savior.* When we lay down the rules and then change them because they are not convenient to enforce at the moment, *we confuse our children and diminish our own credibility.*

Through my own mistakes, I've learned that when our kids are going through necessary developmental stages and we soften their fall . . . well then, we soften *them.* And it hurts them in the long run. It's not such a bad thing to let our kids wrestle through difficult circumstances or to go without something they want, or to face their own character flaws. In fact, all these are necessary for developing healthy, grounded kids.

I don't know about you, but I cringe when I think of who I would be if not for my fumbles and bumbles, and for the painful refining times in my life. And though it will be painful to watch, our children will grow in character and virtue as they struggle through some of life's inequalities.

Though it doesn't always feel this way, there's a limit to what God allows in the life of the believer. He works all things—everything we encounter—for the good, because we love Him and are called according to His purpose (see Romans 8:28). We need not be afraid of hard times because God uses them to shape us (and our kids) into something beautiful.

We need not be afraid of going without because God is faithful, and He will supply all of our needs. What a powerful lesson to impart to our children as soon as they are old enough to understand it! And during those seasons when we don't get to have what we want, God always offers us something so much better, be it insight, clarity, conviction, vision, or character. He is a Master at providing pools of blessings in those dry and weary places (see Psalm 84:6–7).

When we grab for ourselves because we think God won't come through for us, we miss out on a perfect opportunity to see just how good He is. When we overindulge our kids because it seems easier than dealing with their selfishness, everybody loses. And when we pamper ourselves *as a way of life*, we weaken our character and starve the soul.

We work to feed our appetites; Meanwhile our souls go hungry.
(Ecclesiastes 6:7 THE MESSAGE)

Not that it's bad to enjoy an occasional treat. The Bible says that

God gives us all good things to enjoy (see 1 Timothy 6:17)! Fudge brownie sundaes, trendy outfits, and shiny new bikes are all wonderful things that make life especially sweet. God gives great gifts to His children. But the thing is, these are the desserts of life, not the main course. And when we teach our kids to wait on God rather than grab for themselves, we impart to them a virtue worth more than a hundred shiny bikes, a thousand new outfits, or even ten thousand Twinkies.

In this me-first, I-want-what-I-want-and-I-want-it-now generation, may we model and impart the timeless wisdom of patient waiting and gritty self-control.

Since ancient times no one has heard, no ear has perceived, no eye has seen any God besides you, who acts on behalf of those who wait for him. (Isaiah 64:4)

personal application:

- Ask the Lord this question: "What in my life should I lay down that I may take hold of more of You?"

- Based on what God shows you, do a partial fast once a week (give up a meal, a TV show, snacks, coffee, and so on).

- Once a week, say no to yourself as God leads (e.g., refuse to open the bag of chips on the way home from the grocery store; decide not to buy that extra thing you don't need).

parental application:

- Prayerfully ask Jesus for a heightened sensitivity to your children's "addictive" or selfish tendencies. Try the partial fast on them on a small scale at first.

- Take the opportunity to teach your child about the "muscle" of self-restraint. Explain it in those terms. Paint a clear picture of how practicing restraint both strengthens and protects them.

- As they grow in the Lord, ask them if there's anything they would like to volunteer up to God for a day or a week. Prayerfully ask the Lord to help your child own this conviction.

Father in heaven,

Thank You for loving me. Thank You for Your patience and Your grace. Help me to live in a manner worthy of the call on my life. Help me to walk and live and breathe by the Spirit of God within me and not gratify the desires of my flesh. Lord, help me to impart these same truths to my precious little lambs. May they grow up abounding in faith and be totally grateful. Make them strong in conviction and self-control. Help us all to live more like You. Amen.

take time to play

GOD IS GOOD

Because you are my help, I sing in the shadow of your wings.

(PSALM 63:7)

"Our loving God wills that we eat, drink, and be merry."[1]

—MARTIN LUTHER

y mom has a certain gift for hospitality. Unfortunately for her, my strong sense of smell and love for personal space sometimes got in the way of her gatherings. On more than one occasion when she had a few ladies over for dessert, a younger version of myself, I'm told, would crawl under their chairs and put their stinky shoes back on their feet. I guess I was trying to pass along the hint that it was time for them to go home. My poor mom would apologize for my behavior and, of course, send me to my room. I'd receive a talking-to later. Much later, after I had time to think about what I had done.

My parents worked hard to keep a family of nine afloat. Amidst the daily grind of endless laundry and mounds of dishes, my mom still made time to bake cookies, help us fill water balloons, judge our pretend gymnastics meets, allow multiple-friend sleepovers, host neighborhood barbeques, and cook dinner for our large family every night. All of these special moments brought normalcy to our home and provided a constant example of the importance of celebrating life.

One of the fondest memories from my youth was what my brother and I affectionately dubbed as a "blast." Every other weekend one of us asked the other, "Wanna have a blast tonight?" The answer was always an enthusiastic "Yes! Let's do it!" Next we had to get permission. If our parents said yes, we excitedly packed up our sleeping bags and pillows and went down in the basement. We brought down snacks and pillows and books and got all set up for our basement campout. The best part happened when our parents thought we were asleep (or was it when we thought they were asleep?).

Like stealth spies, the two of us quietly crawled up the stairs, shimmied across the floor, and snuck over to the snack cupboard to get more treats. We fell asleep telling each other stories or watching TV (but I only remember a screen full of "bugs" because the programming ended at about midnight). Sometimes my mom helped us build a tent out of blankets, which made our blasts especially fun.

Yesterday I asked my twenty-year-old son Jordan about his favorite childhood pastime. His response first made me cringe and then laugh out loud. "My favorite game was when the brothers and I ran across the living room and Dad tried to take us out by throwing a pillow at our feet."

That game always stressed me out. I couldn't watch it. I'd work in the kitchen and occasionally peek out to the living room to see one of my precious children flying through the air while laughing from the tips of their toes. I'm quite sure that the *try and take out your child by throwing a pillow at his feet* game is now illegal. Of all the fun family games we played, it was the dangerous one that he loved the most. Hmmm.

✿ ✿ ✿

Why is it important not only to play with our children but also to help them engage in their own fun playtimes? Simply said, in both good and bad times, life is a precious gift worth celebrating. We have a capable and loving heavenly Father who carries the world on His shoulders so that we don't have to. When, amidst the stresses of life, we play and laugh and sing with our children, we send them the strong message that ultimately *we believe* that God is in control and that He is faithful.

Engaging in fun times also lets our children know that they are super valuable to us. As human beings, we put our time into the things we care about. And so, when we make time for frivolous fun with our kids, it lets them know that we are honored and blessed to spend our gift of time *with them*.

For parents who love Jesus, making room for fun is like planting seeds of faith in the landscape of our lives. If we take ourselves too seriously, forget to laugh and play, and continually view life through the lens of cable news, we're missing out on some of the best parts of the Christian life.

There, in the presence of the Lord your God, you and your families shall eat and shall rejoice in everything you have put your hand to, because the Lord your God has blessed you. (Deuteronomy 12:7)

We live in trying times, and our culture moves at an unrelenting pace. Our kids witness these realities every day, and it's unsettling to them to say the least. Therefore, when we have the faith to step away from our very important pressing responsibilities and are willing to engage in the fun stuff of life, we send the message to our kids that everything is going to be all right.

When we, right in the midst of economic downturns and budget cuts, have a movie night with buttered popcorn and then we thank God for all He has accomplished through us (and for all the ways He plans on using us in the future), we model to our kids that faith and gratitude are appropriate in all seasons of life.

Not that every activity has to be spiritually driven. We can overdo it in that regard and inoculate our kids from those sacred moments when we really have a chance to speak into their lives about something significant. By the guidance of the Holy Spirit within us, may we have the wisdom to pick and choose those times. Yes, God is in every nook and cranny of life, but as our kids get older, we will push them away if we try to spiritualize every single moment we have with them.

Besides, it's easy to find blessings in typical childhood fun. Water fights, lemonade stands, movie nights, and story times are like streams of refreshment in the dry and weary seasons of life.

We can impart gratitude simply by helping our children understand how blessed we are to enjoy such fun and silly times. God has given us time, space, and everyday items (like nighttime snacks and flying pillows) with which to celebrate life.

The Lord directs the steps of the godly. He delights in every detail of their lives. (Psalm 37:23 NLT)

The Bible says that *every* good gift comes from above (see James 1:17). Every precious drop of life that refreshes us is a gift from our loving Father. Jesus invented water fights and yard games and barbeques and jump rope. He is kind, loving, and generous. He is hilariously wonderful and has a great sense of humor. I'm convinced that we make Him laugh out loud from time to time. He is the wisest and most loving of Fathers and the fiercest and mightiest of protectors. What a treasure it is to have Him in our lives!

Once our children begin to understand the Lord's accessibility and His precious love and care for them, they will embrace the idea that even during playtimes, God is right there, chuckling along with them (unless of course, they start a fire in the sandbox, in which case He stops chuckling and tells Mom that she'd better look out the window. I found that out the hard way).

Take time to play, but don't just play. In your own life, *acknowledge* that every fun moment is a treasured gift from a loving involved heavenly Father. As a parent, copy God's example of how He has

> God has given us **TIME, SPACE** and everyday items (like **NIGHTTIME SNACKS** and flying pillows) with which to **CELEBRATE LIFE.**

parented you. Model this same loving, playful, caring involvement to your children. Laugh with them. Make it easy for them to understand just how wonderful this God of ours is.

Taste and see that the Lord is good; blessed is the man who takes refuge in him. (Psalm 34:8)

Here are a few more ways to engage your children in the celebration of life (memories from author Arlene James's years of raising her children):

FORMAL FUN

On a rainy day, the girls would stage ballet after ballet for us with the boys serving as announcers and musicians, or we would prepare elaborate tea parties, which the boys would attend with paper flowers in hand and wearing bow ties and other "formal" costumes. We awarded them points for their attire, manners, gifts, etc. The winner got to name the next game.

PAPER FIGHTS

The boys' favorite rainy day game was a paper fight. We sat at the dinner table and squashed sheets of paper into "snowballs." When we couldn't keep them on the table anymore, we divided the ammo equally into trash bags, forted up in the living room (removing any breakables) and went to war. Every time someone took a hit, they had to plaster a sticker on themselves. When all the ammo was expended, we counted stickers. The team that took the most hits lost.

WATER FIGHTS

In the summertime we filled water balloons and had the fight outdoors. Those who took hits had to wear safety pins. In both paper and water fights, it was illegal to touch anyone with anything except the "ammo." An infraction of that rule, even accidentally, resulted in the offender receiving a sticker or pin.

PICNIC AT HOME

As they grew older, we developed some traditions: a picnic at home on the first day after the last day of school, even if we had to eat on the floor of the living room due to weather. That continued until our youngest son graduated from high school.

ROAD TRIP STORIES

Whenever we drove any distance in a car together, we read aloud to one another. We took turns, and the reader got to choose the book. (Once, upon being asked by a friend if he had read Sherlock Holmes, my oldest son replied, "I have heard a lot of him.") I'm happy to say that same son has continued that tradition with his daughters.[2]

Delight yourself in the Lord and He will give you the desires of your heart. (Psalm 37:4)

When I was a new believer, the "delight yourself in the Lord" verse made me think of one of the guests at my mom's dessert parties. I pictured her holding up a piece of gum, pointing to her cheek, and in a sugary sweet voice saying, "Give me a kiss and I'll give you this!" As much as I loved chewing gum, I didn't want to kiss a stranger on the cheek.

I couldn't help but wonder—was God so desperate for love and attention that He had to coax me into kissing Him on the cheek before He would give me the things that I wanted in life? Thankfully, I learned after studying this verse, that I couldn't have been more wrong.

The Hebrew translation of the word "delight" is *anag* (pronounced *aw-nag*),[3] which means several things:

- Be pampered
- Be happy about (take exquisite delight in)
- Make sport of

After praying about, cross referencing, and pondering these definitions, I discovered something beautiful about God. This verse reinforced to me how deeply He wants a real and authentic relationship with us. Let's take the three points, one at a time, and see if we can't learn something new about Jesus.

PAMPER YOURSELF—How do you pamper yourself in the

Lord? Think about how you pamper yourself in marriage. You take a break from business as usual and you go on a date, just for the sake of being together. Now think of God. To pamper yourself in the Lord is to spend time with Him for no other reason than to be with Him. I may light a candle, put on some worship music, put my head back and just listen to the words of the song. During that time I remind myself once again how blessed I am to belong to God. Instead of asking for a gift from His hand, I'm more interested in knowing His heart. To delight in the Lord is to spend some time pampering yourself with His presence. And giving yourself some time with Jesus is one of the greatest gifts you can give your children.

BE HAPPY ABOUT—When my husband and I walked through some intense battles with sickness and the financial hardships that followed, we found great joy in both remembering and dreaming together. Several times after arguments about money, when we were exhausted from the stress and strain of it all, we'd sit together on the couch and hold hands. I'd put my head on his shoulder, and we would replay and recount the ways God had come through for us in past trials. With each story we shared, fresh faith emerged. Then we'd move on to dreaming about the future together. We shared our dreams of paid-off medical debt, restored health, a new home, and sons following wholeheartedly after Jesus. This brought joy to our hearts and strength to our souls. Over and over again the Bible reminds us to remember what God has done and to believe Him for what He will do. Part of delighting in the Lord is *remembering with Him,* all of the things you've been through together. And it's also as ones who belong to Jesus, our **FUN TIMES** are so much **SWEETER** when we see them as a gift **FROM HIM.**

about listening to His voice and *dreaming with Him* about all of the ways He wants to work in and through you and your children. A little side note: another priceless gift you can give your children is the ability to search for and find joy in God's perspective regardless of your current circumstances.

MAKE SPORT OF—When I think of a healthy marriage, I think of those essential times of pampering and intimacy, and of those nourishing times of remembering and dreaming together. And finally, no marriage would be complete without occasional and spontaneous fun! Part of delighting in your spouse is to make room to enjoy one another. Moreover, as ones who belong to Jesus, our fun times are so much sweeter when we see them as a gift from Him. When my husband and I bike the trails, I stretch out my arms and say thanks to God out loud. I do. When we go out on our boat and sit in the middle of a lake, I look up at the sky and thank Jesus for such a sacred moment. When we sit out on our deck, sip on iced tea, and laugh about all of the ways we survived raising boys, I smile and thank God once again. Acknowledging God in every fun thing I get to do reminds me that I am His and He is mine, and that every day, He sings a love song over me. Delight in the Lord by acknowledging Him in every enjoyable and special moment of your life. Remember—acknowledging God in your life celebrations brings faith and assurance to your children.

Picture the old woman with more lipstick than lips holding up a piece of gum and pointing to her cheek for a kiss. That's not delight. That's bribery. Now picture your Savior beckoning you to rest in Him, remember with Him, dream with Him, and enjoy life with Him. That's delight. That's what a thriving relationship looks like. What happens when we learn to delight in the Lord? Something amazing happens—*He gives us the desires of our hearts.*

The Hebrew translation for the word "give" in this verse is *nathan* (pronounced *naw-than*).[4]

When I dug deeper into the meaning of this word, it brought all kinds of faith and assurance to my soul. How does Jesus *give* to those who delight in Him? Read some of the words that describe how the Lord gets His good gifts to us:

To give, bestow, grant, permit, ascribe, employ, devote, consecrate, dedicate, pay wages, sell, exchange, lend, commit, entrust, give over, deliver up, yield produce, occasion, produce, requite to, report, mention, utter, stretch out, extend, to put, set, put on, put upon, appoint, assign, designate.[5]

My two favorite words here are *mention* and *utter*. As you and are I busy engaging in life and delighting in the Lord (and entrusting our cares to Him), He *mentions* our name to someone in a position to help us. Maybe that person has the job we need, or a bag of groceries to share, or is in a position of influence to open ministry doors for us. Instead of straining and striving to get our way, we rest in and rely on our God. We delight in Him. And He makes a way for us. That's what it means to *cease striving and know that He is God* (see Psalm 46:10). He knows your name. He knows where you live. And His resources are boundless.

Time and time again, I've used this passage to teach my boys that God knows their name, their address, and the desires of their hearts. As they delight in Him, He will most certainly establish them.

There's no need to compartmentalize our lives, our faith, or our fun, for that matter. All of it matters to God. And when we take time to play with our children and model to them our faith in God, we bring joy to His heart. We delight in Him. He establishes us. Take time to play. God is good.

personal application:

- Pamper yourself in the Lord this week. Put on some music and simply rest. Thank Him for His presence in your life.

- Sit with a friend or your spouse, or even with your child and recount how faithful God has been. Dream about the future.

- This week when you catch yourself laughing or enjoying a moment of peace, pause and remember that every good gift comes from God. Smile at the thought of it. And thank Him. What are your two favorite words from the list of how God "gives" things to you? Really ponder those words in the coming days.

parental application:

- Build a blanket fort with your kids. Snuggle inside with some snacks and good books. Ask them about their dreams.
- Ditch the laundry for a day and take the kids to the park. Swing on the swings and sing a song out loud. Let them see you have fun.
- During bedtime prayers, spend some extra time with your children thanking God for the blessings you enjoy.

Dear Lord,

Forgive me for forgetting just how good You are! You carry the world on Your shoulders so I don't have to. Fill me up today with a fresh assurance of Your love and protection over us. You promised to supply all of our needs; help me to model that faith and assurance to my children. Remind me to slow down and play with them. Open my eyes to how You're working all around us so I can teach my children just how great You are. Amen.

Section Two

TEACH PERSPECTIVE

develop compassion

GOD IS KIND

Therefore, as God's chosen people, holy and dearly loved, clothe yourselves with compassion, kindness, humility, gentleness and patience. **(COLOSSIANS 3:12)**

"Do what you can, with what you have, where you are."[1]

—THEODORE ROOSEVELT

 number of years ago while tossing and turning in bed one night, I asked God to forgive me for all of the bratty things I did as a child. My mom would tell you that I was a sweet girl who tried hard to please people, and I was. She wouldn't say this in front of my brothers and sisters, but I'm pretty sure I was her favorite. ☺ But I also had a snarky side. I was a tomboy with a little bit of feistiness in my bones. I was caring and giving, loving and accommodating. And yet, if someone was mean to me or to someone I loved, that niceness turned to ice, and I came out swinging.

My husband's steady breathing let me know that he was in a deep sleep. But for me, sleep wouldn't come. With my bedsheets tied up in knots and my pillow feeling especially lumpy, I knew this was going to be a long night. I was uncomfortable in bed and uncomfortable with this journey down memory lane, but I knew God was in it, so I followed.

I specifically remembered a time when the neighborhood bully yelled out mean things to my brother and me, and then he threatened to beat us up. Just before we turned to run for our lives, we spouted our own brand of insults intended to hit their mark. And they did. I called the bully a pug nose because he had a big nose, and when he was especially angry, his nostrils flared to the size of saucers.

How could I have said such a terrible thing to such an angry boy? As an adult, it's now obvious to me that this guy had a lot of anguish inside. I grabbed my pillow a little tighter and prayed, "Oh, God, please forgive me for saying such ignorant and painful words! Please, please bless Mike, and heal his wounded heart. Help him to know about Your great love. I'm truly sorry, Lord. What else? Show me more."

For the rest of the night, Jesus gently showed me the times throughout my life that I had been anything but compassionate. Though deep inside I had a fierce heart for the underdog, the teased, and the person at the bottom of the pile, I still had major blind spots when it came to the hurting, the hungry, and the hopeless. Throughout the night, I prayed and asked forgiveness. And the more I prayed, the more hopeful I felt. Clear as the stars shining out my window, I could sense how deeply God wanted His very own love to beat in my heart. And I wanted that too.

To get us ready to grow stronger in faith, first God sets His plow to dig a little deeper in the soil of our hearts. He turns over the hardened soil packed down from ignorance, disobedience, selfishness, unforgiveness, unconfessed sin, and unbelief. He removes the rocks and weeds. And then He plants some new seeds that will eventually produce life—life that blesses us and nourishes others. That's exactly what God was doing with me. In order to grow my heart of compassion and give me eyes to see the world the way He does, He first had to show me just how blind I was.

Even though I didn't like bullies and felt bad for the underdog, my world as a young person was painfully small and without perspective. But God, in His kindness, put people in my path from time to time, people whose convictions opened my eyes to God's enormous heart for the world, and this changed everything for me.

That's what our children need from us. It's not enough to teach our kids to be kind, although kindness in itself is a lost art. We, as the hands and feet of Christ, must intentionally teach our children perspective! We must not be afraid to inform them that 90 percent of the world's population struggles with poverty, oppression, and disease. The painful existence of the underprivileged is far worse than we could ever imagine. Our kids must learn that many, many children will go to bed tonight without one meal in their bellies; that not every homeless person is a lazy drunk; and that children who hurt others are deeply hurt themselves.

Every time we take our children by the hand (in an age appropriate manner), and walk them to the other side of a situation that they might see it from a different angle, we give them the priceless gift of perspective.

When our kids watch movies that make light of racism, disabilities, or faith, we must not be afraid to hit the pause button, point out these blunders, and teach our kids how to discern such things in the future. If you start this early, your kids will be used to the idea that you are the queen of the remote control. But if your kids are older, make no apologies. God has entrusted your children to your care, and you are simply respecting their intelligence enough to teach them how to be critical thinkers. Though they may roll their eyes on occasion, those truths will go in and slowly affect their worldview.

The verse at the beginning of the chapter tells us to clothe ourselves with compassion. We're born naked. Then the nurse wraps us in a blanket. And then our parents take it from there. They put us in outfits that suit their tastes. We dangle along at the mercy of their whims until we get old enough to throw a fit and make some of our own choices about what to wear.

Our children come to us in the same way, and God entrusts us with a beautiful opportunity to shape their thinking while they are young and pliable. We give them a priceless gift if, from the start, we enter into the sufferings of others and take them with us from time to time.

We clothe our children with compassion by teaching them to stop and hold the door for the elderly person walking behind them. We dress them with empathy when we consistently *pray with them* for the hungry and the hurting in our world. We teach them that giving is a way of life when we regularly and sacrificially give in a way that they notice and feel.

When I was in Guatemala, I met a young social worker who was also a mother to a four-year-old little girl. Every few months this young mother of meager means asked her daughter to pick out a couple of toys to bring to a local foster care home. The little girl was so used to this exercise that she thought nothing of it. In fact, she looked forward to these excursions with her momma. Her favorite part of the experience was watching how another child responded to a "new" toy that had become somewhat old to her.

> "I want her to BE SOMEONE who is in the habit of GIVING TO those who have LESS than she has."

About every twelve weeks, the little girl went to her room, squatted down and looked at her toys, and with her finger to her chin, decided which toys she wanted to share with those who had less than she did. Amazingly, she didn't always pick the tired or outdated toy. She often chose a toy that she still liked and thus figured someone else would like it too.

I marveled at this incredible young, single mom. I asked, "You have so little. What compels you to do such a thing with your daughter?" Her response blessed me beyond words, "I want her to keep perspective. I want her to be aware of the needs around her. And I want her to be someone who is in the habit of giving to those who have less than she has."

❀ ❀ ❀

Cultivating compassion in our kids requires initiative and conviction. It's not always an easy thing to do, and it's rarely convenient. In fact, it's much easier—for the moment at least—to cater to the selfish whims of our children, to keep peace rather than plant peace, and to live in a suburban bubble while ignoring the sufferings of those around us.

Our darling, self-centered children love it when life is all about them. But it must not always be. Regardless of their occasional moans and groans, we must interrupt their plans to be selfish and introduce them to the idea that God has a big giant heart for the least of these, and He has entrusted some of the world's needs to our care. We get to be His hands and feet to a lost and dying world! Though it may sometimes be difficult to train our kids in the ways of compassion, eventually, they'll thank us for granting them a much larger worldview.

Fix these words of mine in your hearts and minds; tie them as symbols on your hands and bind them on your foreheads. Teach them to your children, talking about them when you sit at home and when you walk along the road, when you lie down and when you get up. (Deuteronomy 11:18–19)

A fellow author friend of mine, Virginia Smith, wrote a great story about a time when she tried to cultivate compassion in her kids. Read on:

After a long day of Christmas shopping, my adult daughter and I found a table in the food court to rest our aching feet and sip hot cocoa. With sighs of relief, we piled our packages around us and sat back to watch the parade of mall shoppers. Our talk turned to past Christmases.

"Do you remember the year we did Christmas for that poor family?" my daughter asked.

I certainly did! I had become concerned that my ten- and thirteen-year-old children were too self-centered, so we "adopted" a needy family. Our commitment was to provide everything—toys, clothes, even food, for Christmas dinner. The kids helped with shopping and wrapping the gifts, and when they participated enthusiastically, I thought my plan was succeeding.

Then came delivery day—Christmas Eve. We drove to a not-so-nice part of town and parked in front of a rundown trailer. I saw my son's eyes widen as he glimpsed a rust-eaten car with no doors, propped up on cement blocks in the front yard. Rust speckled the tin roof of the trailer as well, and one of the windows had been replaced by cardboard and crisscrossed with duct tape.

The mother of this family had taken the younger kids out, leaving a grandmother and a girl my daughter's age to receive our gifts. Stepping into their tiny living room, I fought to hide my tears at the sight of the smallest Christmas tree I had ever seen, one even Charlie Brown would have rejected. Childish handmade paper ornaments decorated the drooping branches, hung there as beacons of hope that this season of God's abiding love would bring something special to even this humble home. We unloaded bag after bag, and soon we had filled up the single room and covered the kitchen counters. The girl and her grandmother were so grateful we were embarrassed by their constant thanks.

Both of my kids were silent in the car as we drove home, and I was mentally congratulating myself on teaching them a valuable lesson in Christian charity. But then my daughter burst out in an angry voice, "Well, thank you very much for ruining my Christmas! I can't believe you took me to that terrible place." Devastated, I realized my lesson in love had failed.

As I recounted this to my adult daughter, she listened quietly. Then she shook her head. "I don't remember being upset. But I do remember how happy that girl was to get our gifts, and how good it felt to give them. It's one of my best Christmas memories."

As parents, our responsibility is to model God's love for our children. We can't always tell what effect our efforts will have, and sometimes the lesson isn't fully learned until time has done its part in seasoning the message. But when we're obedient, we can trust God to teach the lessons in His own time.[2]

❀
❀
❀

I absolutely love this story! Let's look at Virginia's last paragraph again:

"As parents, our responsibility is to model God's love for our children. We can't always tell what effect our efforts will have, and sometimes the lesson isn't fully learned until time has done its part in seasoning the message. But when we're obedient, we can trust God to teach the lessons in His own time."

One of the things I love about God is that He is faithful. And He cares about this stuff far more than we do! We don't have to do it all. But we do have to be who God intends for us to be (and He wills that we be thriving, whole, healthy, free, and compassionate followers of Christ). *He* will take our little offerings and make something of them. *He* will take the seeds we plant and use the experiences we provide to shape the thinking and perspectives of our children.

Since this is true (in spite of the eye rolls and selfish fits), we have to be brave enough to model conviction and to cultivate an atmosphere where compassion can grow within our families. Picture yourself driving your kids to school and praying out loud, "Dear Jesus, please use us in powerful ways today! Open our eyes to those in need. Help us to be your hands and feet today. Take what we have and make something of it. Help us to live big lives, not selfish ones. We'll be looking for You today! Amen." And then tell your kids, "Look for ways to help others today and then share your stories at dinner tonight." Prayers and plans like this develop a tangible expectancy in our children.

Recently, while paging through a parenting book, I came across a section on teaching empathy to your children. As I read through the author's long list of to-dos, I mentally checked them off in my mind: "Didn't do that. Or that. Not that one either. Oops, missed that one. Didn't do that, or that, or that! Oh, my goodness! What *did* I do to develop compassion in my children?"

For a brief moment, I felt like a failure even though I know my sons have hearts of compassion. I pondered those feelings for a moment, and then I asked myself, why *do* they have compassion? Though I was mostly talking to myself, the Holy Spirit once again walked me down memory lane. Only this time it was a little less painful.

When they were young and I spent far too many months in bed, my boys helped my husband serve *me*. As uncomfortable as it was, I now see that they received hands-on experience in taking care of a sick person. Though I was ill and our finances were scarce, we could pray for the poor and share an occasional box of cereal with someone in need. And pray and share we did. Miniscule as it seems, God moved on those times and used them to shape my sons' lives.

Whenever God blessed us with the opportunity to go to a carnival, an amusement park, or a water park, we paused and reminded our kids how many millions of children will never get to see places like this; not in a guilty way, but in a grateful way. Then we'd thank Jesus and commit the day to Him.

We have a tradition that we carry on to this day. Every Christmas morning we gather down by the tree. Before we open presents, my husband, Kevin, and I share a devotional, and then we spend some time praying for the armed forces and their families, for the poor and the hungry, for the slave and the child-trafficking victim. Our kids are never in a hurry to get through this time of prayer. It's such a perfect way to start Christmas for us. It puts things in perspective. And it helps us remember those who don't get to sit down by a warm fire and open presents on Christmas morning.

Several years ago, my husband and I became involved with the International Justice Mission (IJM), a powerful organization that, among other things, rescues young girls from the horrific life of human trafficking. Each year Kevin and I, along with national recording artist Sara Groves and her husband, Troy, co-chair the IJM benefit in Minnesota. Our sons love this event and now know a lot about the issues of slavery and trafficking in our day. And their lives are different as a result.

Though our efforts didn't seem heroic at the time, God used these things to cultivate within our sons a certain distaste for entitlement, materialism, pride, and selfishness. Beating within them is a heart for the poor, the homeless, and the hurting. Our sons' heroes are not those who can act on the big screen. But they are completely inspired by those who give their lives to help those in need. Praise God for His faithfulness.

Not that we did it all perfectly—far from it—but like the quote at the beginning of this chapter, we did what we could with what we had, and then God took it from there.

> we did WHAT WE COULD with WHAT WE HAD, and then GOD TOOK IT from there.

personal application:

- Daily ask God to awaken His heart of compassion within you, and then look for ways to be His hands and feet.

- Learn about a ministry that works overseas, be it for the hungry, the refugee, AIDS victims, the trafficking victim, child slavery, child soldiers, etc. Sow a few dollars into this ministry and pray regularly for those it serves. Watch out—your heart of compassion will grow before your eyes!

- Ask the Lord for a divine appointment this week. Listen for His voice and follow His lead.

parental application:

- Teach your children about the poor. Share with them some of your ideas about making a difference in this world. Ask them for some ideas. Make a simple plan; one they can get excited about.

- Point out the many blessings that surround your kids. Educate yourself on the sufferings of others that you may be able to lovingly teach perspective whenever you get the chance. [Important note: This is NEVER to be used as a punishment, guilt, or shame tactic; always share from a place of hope and gratitude; impart a sense of holy responsibility. The Bible says that much is required from those of us who have been given much. See Luke 12:48.]

- Watch movies and read books with a message. For example, together watch *Willy Wonka and the Chocolate Factory* and point out the differences between a greedy kid and a grateful one. Spend some time as a family discussing the effects of selfishness. Look through the book of Proverbs and pick out a few verses on selfishness that support your discussion.

Precious Jesus,

My mind cannot fathom the depths of Your love. You are the greatest force in the universe, and yet You deeply and intimately care about every detail of my life. You are compassionate, kind, and gentle. Help me to be that way too. Develop in me a heart that cares for the hurting, give me eyes to see the suffering, and grant me the courage to make a difference in this world. May my children find it easy to understand Your love for the least of these because of the way that I live. Help me to wisely and

develop compassion

lovingly impart conviction and compassion into my precious little lambs. May they grow up to change the world. Amen.

ask for wisdom

GOD IS GENEROUS

*Your hands have made and fashioned me; give me understanding
that I may learn your commandments.* (PSALM 119:73 ESV)

"Rescue me from the person who tells me of life and
omits Christ, who is wise in the ways of the world and
ignores the movement of the Spirit."[1]

—EUGENE PETERSON

y day sped by in a blur with little time to stop and smell the flowers. Mounds of laundry, stacks of dishes, piles of mail, and toys scattered in the house and around the yard kept me hopping from one thing to the next. With my hands immersed in sudsy dishwater, I took a deep breath and stared out the window at the trees responding to the wind. God was whispering, and the trees were clapping their hands. What a beautiful thought.

My sacred moment was suddenly interrupted by loud sobs coming from upstairs. I knew that cry like I knew my own. My strong-willed, highly dramatic, middle son Luke was having a meltdown. After wiping my hands dry, I headed upstairs to find Luke's face buried in a pillow. Between sobs he let out a few words, "I just don't think . . . I don't think I'll know. I caaaaan't do it!"

"What can't you do?" I asked.

"Hear the sound of God's voice!" he spouted. Then he continued, "I just know the devil is going to trick me into being bad, 'cuz he does that a lot. I'm going to think it's God's voice when it's really the devil's voice, and when I do what he says, I'm going to get into troubbbbbble!" He buried his face back into his pillow and cried like the world was coming to an end.

After whispering a prayer for wisdom, I rolled my sweet eight-year-old onto his back and held his chin in my hand. "Listen to me," I said. "Do you know *my* voice?"

Luke swiped his runny nose with his sleeve, blinked back a few tears, and nodded yes.

"How come you know my voice?" I pressed.

"Cuz you're my momma. You live with me and love me. I know what you sound like."

I smiled and then said, "Well, it's the same with God. When you live with Him, spend time with Him, and believe with all your heart that He is crazy about you, you'll know His voice. He loves you and wants what's best for you. Pretend you and I are walking through a forest, and I tell you to stay right by my side because some parts are dangerous, and you could get lost or hurt. At first, you hold my hand and stay close beside me. Then, after a while, you get curious about what you see and what you hear, and you wander off a bit. I call you back, but you wander a little more. Pretty soon there's so much space between us that you can't see me anymore. How easy would it be for someone to slip between us, and trick you or lie to you . . . especially if you're distracted?"

"Real easy," Luke said as he sat up and stared at me.

I continued, "If we allow ourselves to get too busy or distracted with life to the point that we forget about God, we will be easy targets for the devil. It won't be hard for him to trick us, lie to us, or lead us into trouble. The Bible says that he prowls around just looking for someone to devour or confuse. But God has already told us that He is way stronger than the devil, and if we stay by His side, we'll be okay. God doesn't move away from us. We're the ones who move away from Him." (See 1 Peter 5:8.)

Luke seemed to feel better and liked the idea that there was actually a way *not* to be tricked into getting into trouble. Up to this point in his short life, he'd spent enough time in the corner. Luke pressed a little more. "So you're saying that if I stay close to Jesus, I'll learn what He sounds like, and He will help me do the right thing? And then I'll learn how to stay away from the bad choices that get me into trouble?"

I wrapped my arms around my boy and said, "That's exactly what I'm saying. God loves you so much that He *wants* you to hear what He has to say. He knows what's best for you, and He will faithfully lead you if you will faithfully listen to Him."

Dramatic meltdown aside, Luke has carried that lesson with him his whole life. He is now a stable, steady (nondramatic), godly young man. And he deeply values the voice of the Lord within him. May we (and our children) value the voice of God above all else, and may we follow where He leads.

My sheep hear my voice, and I know them, and they follow me.
(John 10:27 ESV)

❀ ❀ ❀

Our sons were sprawled out across our bed, eating popcorn, and enjoying a fun family discussion. My husband and I loved these times. We both had a few thoughts to share with the boys and then we opened it up for a bit of lively discussion. I started, "Boys, suppose there was a bank in town offering free money. All you had to do was show up and ask for it. What would you do?" Of course their eyes widened, and their excitement notched up a level. Jake was the first to speak. "I'd go to the bank and ask for money. Then I'd keep asking."

I flipped open my Bible and said, "God has given us a similar offer but for something worth far more than gold or money. And to tell you the truth, I think this offer is one of the best kept secrets in the Bible. I hardly hear people talk about it." The guys impatiently asked, "What? What is it?" I pointed to James 1:5 and said, "Wisdom. The Bible says that if we lack wisdom or need wisdom, all we have to do is ask for it, and God will supply it in *generous* amounts.

"Wisdom keeps you out of trouble; money cannot always do that. Wisdom helps you in relationships; money cannot do that. Wisdom guides you through hardships, helps you lead, helps you make money, spend money, make life choices, and much, much more. And God *freely* gives it to those who ask. I ask for wisdom many times a day, every day. And like you said, Jake, I keep asking, and

God gives it to me."

Believe it or not, the boys were quite taken with this lesson on wisdom. They still remember it and still ask for wisdom when they need it. Which is often.

If any of you lacks wisdom, he should ask God, who gives generously to all without finding fault, and it will be given to him. (James 1:5)

We need wisdom because every child is different; there is no one-size-fits-all parenting manual. What works on one child may wreck another. And just because we know our child better than anyone else, doesn't mean we know how to parent him or her better than anyone else. We need insight and direction, and we need to be humble enough to ask for it. And when we ask God for something He wants to give us, we can be expectant that He will deliver on His promise and sometimes from the most unexpected places.

We may receive insight from the mouths of our children or from the words on a page or in a song. God might impart direction to us while we work out in the garden, stand in line at the grocery store, or by observing another mother with her children.

And—if we're open to it—Jesus will offer us priceless wisdom through those who've gone before us, be it our parents, our in-laws, or somebody else's grandma. God is always speaking.

> we need **WISDOM** because every child is **DIFFERENT;** there is no one-size-fits-all parenting **MANUAL.**

Oswald Chambers has said that we should always be in a state of expectancy and leave room for God to come in as He likes. May we be wise enough to consistently listen for what He has to say.

✿ ✿ ✿

I remember a time when my kids were young and I'd had it up to my eyeballs with running boys and flying toys. My boys were so physical, and I was so weak and tired from battling Lyme disease that it seemed I never had enough stamina to keep up with them. On this particular day, things whirled around me at a feverish pitch. After one fight too many, I yelled at the boys—that kind of yelling that makes you feel like your veins are bulging—and sent them to their room. I needed a timeout as much as they did. I sat down, wiped my brow, took a deep breath, and asked God for wisdom and patience. More than anything, I didn't want to be a screaming mom. I wanted to be an in-control mom who handled her children's conflicts with order and peace. Or something like that.

When I was finally ready, I went to Jake and Luke's room and knocked on the door. I poked my head in and said, "Boys, can I talk to you for a minute?" I stepped in and continued, "I shouldn't have yelled at you the way I did just now. What you did was wrong, but I was wrong too. Will you please forgive me?"

My stable firstborn son, Jake, shrugged his shoulders and said, "Yeah, sure. I'm sorry too, Mom." My strong-willed middle son

God doesn't **FAULT US** for asking for **WISDOM**; in fact, He **LOVES** it when we do.

waited his turn to speak, and then on cue he threw his head back, burst into tears, and screamed, "You coulda killed me, you hurt my heart so baaaaaaaad!" Hmmm. Talk about two very different responses to the same incident.

After that, I did my best to tailor my responses to the emotional makeup of each of my boys. Not that I relaxed my standard; I just changed my approach. I didn't do it all at once, but little by little, one step at a time, one prayer for wisdom at a time, the Lord showed me how to parent each child in way that helped him to grow up to be the guy Jesus wanted him to be. God doesn't fault us for asking for this kind of wisdom; in fact, He loves it when we do.

We also need wisdom because we are still works in progress. Without wisdom, we will not only parent by reaction to our circumstances, we will also parent through the filter of our own hang-ups. Again, we cannot impart something we ourselves do not possess. Unless we earnestly press the Lord for wisdom for our broken areas, we will parent in reaction to our fears and insecurities rather than in response to the guidance of the Holy Spirit within us.

Many moms and dads parent out of reaction to the moment, but truly effective moms and dads parent in response to the bigger picture of what God is doing all around them (more on this later).

Just how do we identify our hang-ups? Most of us know right away where we get tripped up. But if you're someone who cannot pinpoint the obstacles and roadblocks to your emotional stability, ask your husband, or your best friend. They'll tell you.

If we keep God at a distance and dismiss our own need for wisdom regarding some of our personal "stuff," we will miss out on the abundant, free life God intended for us. Furthermore, our parenting will suffer because we'll be operating out of our lack rather than from the abundance of what God has offered us. Instead of responding to His voice of wisdom within us, we will react to our child's experiences especially when they are reminiscent of our own fears and insecurities.

Below are a few reaction filters (through which you view your own child's experiences) that are common for us moms, and if not dealt with, they will skew our perspectives and keep us from being the godly, healthy, and wise moms we were meant to be!

REJECTION FILTER: Maybe you endured relentless teasing as a child or cruel rejection from friends or family members. Those experiences, if not dealt with, may leave a filter through which you view your own children's experiences. You'll be tempted to rescue them from the slightest hint of relational difficulty so they will not have to feel the pain that you did. You may be tempted to control the atmosphere (have everything at your house under your rules) so as not to expose them to the slightest possibility of rejection. If and when they do endure the cruelty of others, it re-injures you in a way not proportionate to the incident. Their acceptance feels like a consuming issue for you.

WISDOM SAYS: Deal with this head on! Seek counsel from a godly counselor, pastor, or prayer partner. Every single day remind yourself that YOU are the object of God's affection. People don't get to decide your worth (or your child's), because God already has.

Memorize Scripture that affirms who you are in Christ. Daily reject rejection! Daily declare that there is a wide gap between how people affect you and how God affects you. His voice matters most. As God frees you from these past experiences, you will be better equipped to help your children navigate through the *normal* relational difficulties that take place in childhood. You'll teach them how to love and forgive and to know who they are—this is all the stuff of growth and maturity. And you'll have a much clearer picture of when the situation truly calls for your intervention.

FEAR FILTER: If you experienced a traumatic incident when you were young, or if your mom or dad imparted fear to you by constantly voicing all of the terrible things that *could* happen if you did this or that, you may have a fear filter still in place. The temptation for you will be to hover over your children and not let them take too many risks. You may perpetuate that same fear in them by voicing all of the "what could happen" fears in front of your children. While they are young, they may comply, and you may feel you've done your part by teaching them to be safe in this very controlled environment. But as they age, those fears will manifest in different ways that keep them from taking the necessary risks involved in growing up.

WISDOM SAYS: Again, deal with this head on! Seek counsel from a godly counselor, pastor, or prayer partner. Stand strong in the face of fear. Voice your faith instead. One of my favorite verses on fear is Isaiah 8:13–14 (NLT, 1996 edition): "Do not fear anything except the Lord Almighty. He alone is the Holy One. If you fear him, you need fear nothing else. He will keep you safe." Fear looks at life without God in mind, and yet, this God that we serve is mighty and strong and true. A gazillion things *could* happen, but many never will. Fear opens the door to worry. Fear keeps us from going to the Promised Land places God has for us. Fear cripples us, and faith sets us free. Fight this battle and put fear under your feet. Let your children see you be victorious! Speak to them about the *possibilities* of *what could happen* if they dared take God at His word.

WORRY AND ANXIETY FILTER: This one is similar to the fear issue. If you grew up hearing your mom voice all of her "what if" fears and worries, and those same fears got under your skin, you may have inherited a worry filter. If, as a child, you spoke out all of your worries, and no one redirected you to God's faithfulness, you may still have a bent toward worry and anxiety. The tendency here is to unknowingly pass down the worry filter to your children. If, with every mishap and interruption, your children see your stress level go up and your perspective go out the window, they will absorb your stress and your perspective. Furthermore, they will come to believe they are at the mercy of all of the "what-ifs" out there, and this can make them feel especially insecure.

WISDOM SAYS: Again, deal with this head-on! Seek counsel from a godly counselor, pastor, or prayer partner. The Bible gives us a clear directive regarding worry, which means we have an actual choice in the matter: "Do not be anxious about anything, but in everything, by prayer and petition, with thanksgiving, present your requests to God. And the peace of God, which transcends all under-standing, will guard your hearts and your minds in Christ Jesus" (Philippians 4:6–7).

In this day of global instability, we do have plenty to worry about, and yet, God clearly exhorts us to turn our backs on worry. In *every* situation, He has made a way for us. A stable, trusting heart is one of the best gifts we can give our children. When we hang on to peace, we more easily pass it along to them.

PRIDE AND PRESENTATION FILTER: Maybe you grew up learning that appearances, clothes, and possessions are defining factors for you. Perhaps you believe status to be of utmost impor-tance. You can't help yourself, but you look down on those who don't have it quite as together as you. You work hard to make sure your kids have the latest and greatest of everything. And you like to be associated with other families who share your affinity for a polished appearance. Or, conversely, maybe while growing up you battled with the worry of wondering if your daily personal needs would be met, and this caused great stress in your world. As a result, your pendulum has swung the other way, and you are determined that your current family life will bear no resemblance to your former life. Either way, the outward presentation matters way too much to you, and rather than raise your children to bear the image of Christ, your efforts serve to shape them into the image of someone who has it all together.

WISDOM SAYS: Volunteer at a homeless shelter. Hand out bowls of soup to those who need a meal. Read the gospels and pay attention to who Jesus hangs out with; follow Him to the slums as He ministers to the least of these. Ask God to set you free from the bondage of appearance that you might be available to serve Him wherever He leads. Every time you're tempted to lift a finger to "impress" instead of bless, refuse the temptation and ask God what He'd have you do. Ask God to make His love and acceptance real to you. Teach your children about how much God loves the hurting and the hungry. And for a complete overhaul, read the book *Same Kind of Different As Me*,[2] by Ron Hall and Denver Moore (it'll make you think).

Just what does our personal freedom have to do with growing grateful kids? While they are still young, our children will most likely NOT thank us for being emotionally free and healthy, or even notice if we're not. However, by embracing God's wisdom for our own spiritual and emotional health, we will become conduits for the freedoms of others, namely, our children. By pulling up the weeds of past negative influences, we will cultivate an atmosphere where our kids can grow into the fullness of who *they* were meant to be.

Though initially our kids won't be able to articulate why home is a good place to be, they'll just know that it is. And as they get older and they observe the painful home lives of some of their friends, they'll eventually thank us, in their own way, for parenting from a place of wholeness and wisdom.

*Teach me to do your will, for you are my God; may your good
Spirit lead me on level ground.* (Psalm 143:10)

personal application:

- Spend some time reading and praying the verses from Psalm 139:23–24 (take some time to listen to the things God has to say).

- Consider the forest analogy at the beginning of the chapter. Is there a big distance between you and Jesus? Reconnecting with Him is only a prayer away. Spend some time pondering the idea that He really, truly loves you and wants what's best for you.

- Memorize James 1:5 and get in the habit of asking for fresh wisdom daily.

parental application:

- I got this idea from a friend: I explained to my kids that having the Holy Spirit inside us is like having a conscience box within us. When we step off track, the box turns and the sharp corners prick us inside. If we mind those checks and do the right thing, the corners stay sharp. But if we ignore those nudges, like sandpaper in the soul, the corners get rounded off and pretty soon we don't even feel conviction anymore. Teach your children about the conscience box. Help them to understand why we need the voice of the Holy Spirit within us. Help them to value the gift of conviction.

- You will encounter those times when even though you told your children they could go somewhere or had permission to do something, you suddenly felt that lack of peace and unsettledness. Bring those feelings before the Lord. Ask Him to show you whether you are parenting out of "reaction to your hang-ups," or if He is specifically directing you to change plans for their protection. If you strongly sense that God is directing you, then exercise your right as a godly parent to explain how God moves and speaks to us for our guidance and protection. Obey the voice of the Lord, change the plans, and thank Him for His involvement in your life. Eventually, your children will come to appreciate that you have a living, active walk of faith.

• Pray with your kids and ask God to give them abundant amounts of wisdom, wisdom beyond their years. When those words go into their ears, their hearts will beat with expectancy.

Precious Lord,

Your Word calls me to ask for wisdom, and so I ask: Please, Lord, fill me to overflowing with insights from above; grant me a perspective that can only come from You. Help me to stay in step with You in such a way that Your voice is easy for me to recognize. Heal me from the effects of my past; give me a strong sense of Your heart for my children, and help me to raise them up to be everything You intend them to be. Amen.

live humbly

GOD IS GREAT

Humble yourselves, therefore, under God's mighty hand,
that he may lift you up in due time. (**1 Peter 5:6**)

"It was pride that changed the angels into devils;
it is humility that makes men as angels."[1]

—ST. AUGUSTINE OF HIPPO

om! Guess what I found out today?" My third grader Luke burst through the door to share his exciting news.

"What did you find out today, Luke? Tell me!"

With arms flailing and eyes wide, Luke continued, "I found out that *five* kids in my class are Christians. And the janitor is a Christian too."

Knowing my son like I do, I cringed a little and asked, "Hmmm. And how did you find this out?"

With a load of confidence and his hands on his hips, he said, "Oh, that was easy. We were in single file walking to the library, and I was in the front of the line. While we were walking down the hallway, I just stopped, turned around, and made an announcement."

In my mind's eye I pictured Luke turning around in a moving line and causing a train wreck of little people. Luke continued, "I just said—out loud so everyone could hear me—'Okay, people! People listen! Besides me, who all here is a Christian?' And then I watched as different kids in my class put their hands in the air. I pointed to each of them and started to count out loud, 'You, you, you, oh and that makes four.' Even the janitor who was walking by raised his hand. But when Johnny raised his hand, I wasn't sure about him so I said, 'Oh, Johnny, I don't know about you. I've seen you on the playground. You might want to go ask your mom.'"

First I chuckled, then I gasped. Definitely not the ideal mom-response. I stepped in a little closer, "Luke, it's not up to you to tell someone if they are a Christian or not. I'm glad you want to know who in your class is following Jesus, but there are better and gentler ways of going about this." We then sat down and had what would be one of many talks about love and humility and graciousness.

In his book *12 Steps for the Recovering Pharisee*, author John Fischer wrote:

> I am the worst sinner I know, simply because I know myself better than anyone. My sin is the worst because it is mine. I am intimately involved with it. I know all its subtle nuances, its illusions, its rationalizations, and its cover-ups. *Of my sin I am an expert. Anyone else's sin is not my business to evaluate.*[2] (Emphasis mine)

Luke was like a bulldog in many ways, but yet so loving and

tender at the same time. He had asked Jesus to be his Savior earlier that year. I remember the moment like it was yesterday. We were on our way home from a baseball game (another one of my fruitless attempts to help Luke get some exercise). Luke was dirty from head to toe—but not because he was so involved in the game. He was dirty because he got bored in the outfield and decided to sneak up to the infield and roll around in the dirt so he could look like the rest of the players.

We pulled into the driveway after the game, and I looked over at my pseudo baseball player whose chubby cheeks were covered in dirt. With his big blue eyes he looked up at me and started in with questions about Jesus and heaven and hell. It took me a few minutes to realize that he managed to interject the word "hell" into every one of his questions and comments.

He said things like, "So . . . about hell. Will everyone who is in hell hate it there?" And, "What do *you* know about hell?" That boy used the word *hell* more times in one conversation than I had in my whole life. It's like he wanted to sow his wild oats before he was ready to leave his wayward ways and follow Jesus. But when he was finally ready, he bowed his head, folded his hands, and prayed the sweetest prayer I'd ever heard. It was a great day.

Later that night when the kids were supposed to be sleeping, I heard Jordan and Luke chattering in their bedroom. Jordan was on the bottom bunk and Luke was on the top bunk. Just when I was about to set my book down and go tell them to stop talking and get to sleep, Luke came down the hall leading Jordan by a fistful of his pajamas. Luke—in his all-too-confident way—said to my husband

and me, "Mom, Dad, JoJo doesn't want to go to hell either. Pray that prayer with him that you prayed with me today." And to that, our sweet little Jordan added, "Yeah. What he said."

In his younger years, Lukey was much like the disciple Peter. He came on strong, had lots of passion, and got himself into trouble on occasion. Though some of his too-big-for-his-britches attitudes had to be harnessed and redirected at times, I suppose he was in good company.

> "The remarkable thing is not that I sin, but that, in spite of my sin, I am capable of having fellowship with God and being used by him for his purposes in the world."[3]

One of my favorite stories in the Bible is the Old Testament account of Joseph. Amidst incredible injustice, false accusations, and misassigned motives, Joseph walked humbly with God and embraced a lifestyle of honor. And in each difficult situation, he found favor with God and with his superiors. Like the cream that rises to the top, Joseph rose to a place of influence in every season of life, regardless of the hardship leveled against him.

Joseph allowed God to refine him through difficult times, which made him ready to lead a nation in need. He started out as a young man with a big dream and immaturely bragged about it to his already jealous brothers. But over time, God harnessed Joseph's passion, refined his character, and made him ready for greatness.

Joseph did more than get by; he flourished amidst his trying times. He managed to guard his heart against bitterness and pride, and he learned from his humbling experiences. He was an amazing man, and his life models for us the verse at the beginning of this chapter. He humbled himself under the mighty hand of God; in the face of painful and brutal circumstances, he didn't get bitter or rebellious or prideful. He entrusted himself to God, and, in due time, the Lord lifted him up and blessed him before a watching world.

Samson of the Old Testament was also a young man with a mighty call on his life. But that's where the similarities end. Though Samson was gifted and called by God, he refused to listen to his parents; he repeatedly neglected wisdom and arrogantly took matters into his own hands. He was reactionary, bullheaded, and spoiled. Just imagine how different his life would have been had he embraced his vow to God not just on the surface but also in the depths of his being.

Samson's life reminds us that it's not enough to have unique gifts from God and a special call on our lives. We must earnestly desire God's wisdom and direction in the way we steward those gifts. And we must be humble enough to *submit to God* amidst the character cleansing seasons He allows us to endure. In fact, I think it's dangerous to have a strong sense of your gifts without a humble dependence upon God to keep you on track. Samson's life tragically illustrates that point.

What do painful refining times and a humble, reliant heart have to do with raising grateful kids? Everything! Our kids *learn* by watching us. If they see us flaunting our gifts as if we own them and living in a way that magnifies us and not God, our children will inherit a skewed view of the Almighty. They will consider Him a side note in life and not the Savior we know Him to be. Jesus is great and wonderful, awesome and true. And we are orphans who've been adopted, saved, restored, and set free. We have nothing to boast in except the fact that we are loved and adored by our Creator. What a lofty responsibility we have in raising our children! Lord,

what do painful refining times and a **HUMBLE, RELIANT HEART** have to do with raising grateful kids? **EVERYTHING!**

help us to live what we believe!

We're not going to do it all perfectly. In fact, we'll make plenty of mistakes along the way. That's why I'm so very thankful for the fresh, new mercies waiting at my door each morning.

Because of the Lord's great love we are not consumed, for his compassions never fail. They are new every morning; great is your faithfulness. (Lamentations 3:22–23)

Even so, our consistent choices are not without consequence; they cause a ripple effect all around us, namely, in the lives of our children. Remember, we can't impart something we ourselves do not possess. What consistent lessons on pride and humility do your kids pick up by *watching* you?

IF OUR KIDS SEE
us shaking our fists at people more than they see us praying for them

THEY'LL LEARN

that people shouldn't get in the way of what we want. That's pride.

IF OUR KIDS SEE

us responding humbly to the rude person in line at the grocery store

THEY'LL LEARN

that we are alive to reflect the character of Christ. That's humility.

IF OUR KIDS SEE

us dissecting others' flaws more than they hear us honoring them in their absence

THEY'LL ACQUIRE

an exaggerated view of their own importance and the idea that it's okay to gossip. That's pride.

IF OUR KIDS SEE

us speaking well of others, giving people the benefit of the doubt, and believing the best about others' motives

THEY'LL LEARN

not to be quick to judge or to assign motives; they'll learn to believe and hope for the best in others. That's humility.

IF OUR KIDS SEE

us striving and straining in our own strength and neglecting to give Jesus the credit He deserves

THEY'LL LEARN

that more rests on our shoulders than on His. They'll come to believe that they are stronger than they really are (and that God is weak in some way). That's pride.

IF OUR KIDS SEE

us humbly committing each new day to Jesus

THEY'LL LEARN

that He truly loves and cares about every detail of our lives. That's humility.

IF OUR KIDS SEE

us disrespecting authority, criticizing our pastor, nitpicking our neighbor

THEY'LL LEARN

that it doesn't matter if Jesus told us to respect authority and to love our neighbor, because our opinions matter more than the things He has asked of us. And that's pride.

IF OUR KIDS SEE

us refusing to forgive, stiffening up in the face of correction, or refusing to admit when we're wrong

THEY'LL HAVE

a front row seat to watch pride in action; they'll fear correction (rather than embrace it); they'll learn to defend their "right" not to grow into everything God intended them to be. That's pride.

IF OUR KIDS SEE

us admitting when we're wrong, asking forgiveness, and applying ourselves to the pursuit of holiness

THEY'LL LEARN

to follow in our footsteps, to admit when they're wrong, to ask for forgiveness, and to apply themselves to the pursuit of holiness. That's humility.

We told our sons from the time they were little that pride is the most insidious attitude anyone can embrace (and we went after it in them like any other act of disobedience or disrespect). It's the very thing that got Satan kicked out of heaven. Pride looks bad, it smells bad, and it breeds dysfunction in every relationship it touches. Pride is rooted in such an evil and basic misunderstanding of God that He actually distances Himself from the proud, but He draws near to the humble (see James 4:6). God hates pride because it is rooted in arrogance, and it separates us from Him. Pride is based on a lie. Embracing pride means we've forgotten who God is.

So, if you think you are standing firm, be careful that you don't fall! (1 Corinthians 10:12)

The other night, my husband and I stood out on the deck and surveyed the newly cut lawn. My husband considers his lawn a work of art. And when the sprinklers come on, he jokingly puts his hands in the air like he's conducting a symphony. When the water sprays through the trees it's like music to his ears. I tease him often about his earnest lawn-care ways, but truth be told, he grooms a pretty nice lawn. As we stood on the deck, he pointed to the grass and said, "You see how thick and full our grass is? The best weed killer in the world is a healthy lawn." I never knew that, but isn't it just like God to design things that way?

If most of our choices reflect a *healthy, growing* walk of faith, those very choices will choke out the impact of our occasional parenting mistakes and mess-ups (as long as we humbly acknowledge those mistakes and make things right whenever possible). Furthermore, it's important for our kids to eventually find out that we need Jesus' sacrifice on the cross just as much as they do. We are most certainly going to make our share of mistakes. Our kids will *see us* blow it from time to time. But hopefully, more often than not, they will *see us* earnestly pursuing God, receiving His mercy, and relying on His strength. May they see us consistently humble ourselves before the Lord, and by watching us, may they learn that *He* is the Source of all we could ever want or need.

We don't have it all together. We simply won't until we see Jesus face to face. Every once in a while, we'll think petty, catty thoughts and we'll react in ways that are beneath us. God knows all of this and cherishes us still. Isn't that just absolutely amazing? How much better for our kids to know the *truth* about us, and the *truth* about God's love, than to have some illusion that we wear a cape and can leap buildings in a single bound.

Eventually that house of cards will tumble down, and we'll have much to deal with if we've contributed to that illusion. Though it's important for our children to look up to us, respect us, rely on us, and be able to trust us . . . part of raising them *to stand* is to slowly help them shift their focus from hoping in *us*, to hoping in and relying on Jesus.

Moreover, pumping our kids full of self-confidence in the absence of a humble respect for God sets them up to fall flat on their faces too (see Proverbs 16:18). If, instead of cultivating a holy confidence and a humble fear of God, we plant within them un-holy seeds of *self-confidence*—and the idea that everything they say is brilliant—we expose their character to a weed that will wrap itself around all that God wants to do in and through them. And if given time to sprout, that self-weed will be tough to uproot later in life.

When I was in college, I had a friend who was supergifted and yet a supremely insecure human being. One day I just blurted out the question, "How is it that you can be so gifted and yet so totally self-aware and insecure?" His answer about knocked me over. "I came from a great family; a Christian family. My mom loved me, and I knew it. But according to her, I could do no wrong. She praised every single thing I did. And if I messed up, she helped me find a reason, or an excuse, or some way to explain why it really wasn't my fault. I went through my school years thinking I was always right. Better than everyone else.

"As you can imagine, I was not at all prepared for what was waiting for me in the real world. Out there, people don't sing your praises every single moment. Bosses don't assume you had the best motive in the world when you mess up. Your professors couldn't care less if you have five good excuses for not doing what they asked. I've encountered more conflict and more disappointment than I know what to do with. It's like I've lost my footing. I don't even know who I am anymore."

Our kids aren't perfect. Jesus needed to die for them too. Furthermore, pride isn't cute, and it's *not* a sign of inner strength. It's truly a horrible seed that creates distance between God and us. Uprooting sin in the lives of our kids is sometimes like delicate surgery. That's why we as parents need to be loving and kind on a regular basis. Then, when it comes time to say the hard thing to our kids, they will believe that in good times and in bad, we are completely in their corner. It's like building equity in their character. We catch them doing things right, we bless them for being kind, and then when it is merited, we confront them for sinful attitudes, average efforts, and lazy thinking. We don't take the easy route; we take the right one, by God's grace.

Growing grateful, humble kids means we must be unsympathetic to *any* attitude that threatens to ruin our children or separate them from God. When we see our children display prideful attitudes such as disrespect, cruelty to other children (namely siblings), teasing others for having less, bragging because they have more, *we need to rise up* and deal with it on the spot.

How can we accomplish this task? First, we ask for wisdom, that the Holy Spirit might show us (and them) what lie our child is embracing to behave the way he or she did. And then, we need to prayerfully and carefully help uproot that lie from his or her life. Does your daughter think she's better than someone else? Does your son think he's entitled? More deserving? As parents, it's part of our duty to lovingly sit with our kids and help them uproot these weeds in their yard.

Regular, honest, and loving conversations help turn over the hardened soil in the hearts of our kids. Tears of forgiveness soften

regular, honest and **LOVING CONVERSATIONS** help turn over the **HARDENED SOIL** in the hearts of our kids.

the soil. And at that moment, you have a perfect atmosphere for planting truth and a fresh perspective.

To live a God-fearing, humble life puts feet to our faith. It shows that we really believe what the Bible says about God and about us. Nothing will teach our kids the reality of God like seeing their parents humbly acknowledging His greatness every single day.

One final note: don't confuse passivity with humility. Passivity sometimes *looks* like meekness or humility. But passivity comes from a self-protective, insecure mind-set. Passivity pays a great price later to avoid discomfort today. Humility, on the other hand is rooted in strength and grounded in the knowledge that the God who holds the earth between His fingers loves and adores me. Humility firmly declares that Christ defines me, and, therefore, I will humbly follow Him and trust Him forever.

Though the Lord is on high, he looks upon the lowly, but the proud he knows from afar. (Psalm 138:6)

personal application:

- Ask God for a heightened sensitivity to help you spot evidences of pride in your own character.

- When you're tempted to impress rather than bless, stop yourself, and ask God what lie you are believing at the moment. Ask Him to give you a fresh perspective of the truth.

- Start each new day on your knees and tell Jesus that you want Him to influence every area of your life. Commit your kids, your husband, and your life to Him. Tell God that you trust Him.

parental application:

- Regularly point out the stark contrasts between pride and humility when watching TV shows, post-game interviews of athletes, etc. Cultivate within your kids an appreciation for humility (and a distaste for pride).

- Always consider disrespect and a bad attitude as something that deserves your immediate attention and intervention.

- When you pray with your child in the morning and in the evening, consistently acknowledge the power, protection, and provision of God. Also, acknowledge your family's utter dependence on Him.

Precious Lord,

I humbly come before You and declare that You alone are God. You are great, and You do marvelous deeds. Thank You for loving me and for walking with me through my everyday life. Fill me with a greater awareness of Your presence that I may live a life fully devoted to You. You are amazing, God. I will follow You forever. Amen.

embrace contentment

GOD IS ENOUGH

Keep your lives free from the love of money and be content with what you have, because God has said, "Never will I leave you; never will I forsake you." **(HEBREWS 13:5)**

"True contentment is a real, even an active, virtue—not only affirmative, but creative. It is the power of getting out of any situation all there is in it."[1]

—*G.K. CHESTERTON*

 y life stunk. At least that's what I thought. I looked up at the IV bag hanging from our broken mini-blinds. My eyes followed the tube down to my arm and then to my hand. I noticed the varying shades of red and some bruising from my previous catheter sites. I was in my twenties, but I felt like I was ninety. I rolled over onto my left side and looked up at the garage sale clothes hanging from a rope that was draped across our living room. Our dryer was broken. Where in the world would we find the money to repair our dryer? I breathed a heavy sigh and looked up at the old rope strung across our living room. I stared at my kids' ratty clothes and

wondered if we'd ever have enough money to buy name brand any-thing. Our house was falling apart. We owed many thousands of dollars in medical debt. I battled Lyme disease while my husband worked two and three jobs to keep food on the table.

My friends made life look easy. They had beautiful homes, dependable cars, and nice clothes. They went out to dinner on occasion and even enjoyed a bit of travel. Best of all, they had their health. I always marveled when I called to see how they were doing, and more often than not they'd reply, "Great!"

I couldn't imagine waking up six out of seven days a week feeling healthy, normal, and strong. In the depths of my being I wanted the kind of lives they lived.

My pity party was set. All I needed was a party hat and some food. Just when I was about to let my mind take another detour, the front door burst open, and my giant of a husband stepped into the entry way and said, "I'm hoooome!" Like a big bear that found his favorite back-scratching tree, he bounded in the door with glee. All of the sudden I heard a loud *thump!* I lifted my head from the couch to look down to the entryway only to find Kevin standing in a gaping hole up to his armpits!

Seconds after Kevin stepped in the door, the floor beneath him gave way, dropping him through a sizeable hole in our entryway. He looked as shocked as I was. With his arms in the air, and his feet in the downstairs closet on a pile of boxes, he looked up at me, and then down at himself, and then up at me again. He was at a loss for words.

We burst out laughing at the same time and couldn't stop (it was either that or break down and cry). Still hooked up to my IV, I leaned over so he could see me from the entryway, and I spouted, "We are pathetic losers! We live in the money pit!" Kevin laughed, shook his head, and climbed out of the hole in the entryway.

Within a few minutes he was out in the garage looking for a piece of plywood to cover up our gaping hole. I pulled out my journal and started to write what was on my heart. I actually surprised myself. Here is a paraphrase of what I wrote that day:

Thank you, Lord, that we have a roof over our head. And thank You, Lord, that we have running water we can freely drink any time of the day. Thank You for food in the cupboards. Thank You that I have a husband who comes home every night. He could so easily abandon us in this whole mess, but day after day he stays and he loves. Thank You, Lord, that we have three little ones playing in the bedroom down the hall who don't even know that we're in the crisis of our lives. They just know they're loved. Thank You, Lord, for loving us like You do. And though my eyes can't see it, I know You will make a way through this terrible time. I know that one day our lives will be better, and things won't feel so hard. You are good, and You will come through for me.

I closed my journal, sat up, and looked out the window. I was the richest woman alive. At that very moment, I had everything I needed to thrive. I lacked no good thing.

But every time (before and after that day) that I committed the sin of comparison and acquired my perspective by looking at what *others* possessed . . . I became the poorest woman alive.

But giving thanks is a sacrifice that truly honors me. (Psalm 50:23 NLT)

❀ ❀ ❀

Though my friends were blessed with financial stability and good health, they had their share of trials and struggles. They didn't skate through life unscathed by the kinds of pain and heartache the rest of us encounter. Even though their lives looked perfect to me, I knew these friends well enough to know that they were honest-to-goodness Christ-followers who trusted God to meet all of their needs and lead them in the way they should go.

Problem was, I made the mistake of comparing my messy looking "insides" to their perfect looking "outsides." And every time I did that, I came up short, I diminished my own value, and I subtracted something from these very special friendships.

The sin of comparison triggers two kinds of responses from us: pride and/or despair—both of which lead us away from our rightful posture of holy confidence and humble dependence. If we compare ourselves to someone who struggles with an issue that happens to be a strength area for us, we will be tempted toward pride (and we'll wonder why they can't just get it together).

And if we compare ourselves to someone who is strong and gifted in an area where we are messy and weak, we'll be tempted toward despair (and we'll wonder what is wrong with us! Why can't we just get it together?).

Whenever we look to the right or to the left and compare ourselves with others, we'll perceive things through a skewed lens. That's why Jesus wants us to spend most of our time looking up. He is writing a beautiful story with our lives. His will for us is our best-case scenario. He doesn't want us to want someone else's story . . . because ours fits us perfectly. What a shame to throw the book across the room because we don't like the chapter we're living at the moment!

To be content is to trust that God is great and that He is always up to something good.

Looking *up* for perspective keeps us more focused on God's strength than on our weakness. Comparing ourselves to others keeps us chained to an earthbound perspective. Until we see Jesus face to face, we will only see in certain shades and hues, and we'll only perceive with partial information.

Our clearest picture will always come through Jesus. When we look at others through Jesus' perspective, it will be easier for us to love them, see the best in them, and care for them in a way that matters. When we look at ourselves through Jesus' perspective, we'll have a deeper understanding of our value, our purpose, and the idea that we truly matter to God. When we survey our situation in light of God's Word, we'll find more tangible hope, gritty faith, and a contentment that defies our circumstances.

On the other hand, if we forget to look up and only look out, we will subject ourselves to the devil's attempts to lure us away from God's promise of peace and contentment. Discontentment compels

> what a shame to throw **THE BOOK** across the room because we don't like **THE CHAPTER** we're living at the **MOMENT!**

us to compare. And when we compare, our conclusions end up being greatly deficient of truth and redemption.

For now we see in a mirror dimly, but then face to face. Now I know in part; then I shall know fully, even as I have been fully known. (1 Corinthians 13:12 ESV)

Contentment (or lack thereof) has little to do with our circumstances and everything to do with what we tell ourselves about those circumstances. In her wonderful book *Calm My Anxious Heart,* Linda Dillow writes this about redirecting our focus that we may learn to live contented lives:

Each of us has a choice about how we look at life: We can focus on the mud or lift our eyes and see the stars. Every woman has circumstances that appear to be prison bars. God wants you and me to learn to be content in our circumstances, not when they improve.[2]

Jesus knows us intimately and loves us profoundly. He gives us perspective. He fuels us to love others. He helps us to find joy in our circumstances. And He compels us to hope for better days.

Many are asking, "Who can show us any good?" Let the light of your face shine upon us, O Lord. You have filled my heart with greater joy than when their grain and new wine abound. I will lie down and sleep in peace, for you alone, O Lord, make me dwell in safety. (Psalm 4:6–8)

❀ ❀ ❀

Children learn what they live. And if they live with parents who are never satisfied, always striving, ever looking for the next best thing to feed their material appetites—then those children will come to believe that life comes from *stuff*. And stuff breaks down, gets old, is outdated in a matter of hours, or simply doesn't satisfy for very long. As a result, those kids will hunger and thirst and yearn for *more stuff*. Different stuff. But more stuff, nonetheless.

The job of teaching our children contentment in this self-entitled, materialistic, me-first culture is uniquely ours as parents. If we don't sow seeds of contentment or actively provide perspective when our kids are young, our children will likely grow up with one of two schools of thought: *I need the stuff*: They will run fast and hard after the stuff—and often on a bigger scale than their parents did. Or, *I hate the stuff*: They will acquire conviction for a simpler life and a desire to help those in need; and they'll lose a measure of respect for parents who were too shallow to teach them such principles.

Again, not that we're going to sow every potential seed or seize every perfect opportunity, but may we live close enough to the Father's heart that we hear His voice when He whispers to us, *"Be thankful in this moment,"* or *"You don't need to buy that today,"* or *"Don't look too long at your neighbor's stuff. Come and spend some time with Me instead, and I will give you peace."*

What's the opposite of such God-responses? Whining. Complaining. Grumbling. Comparing. Buying. Eating. Spending. Charging. Striving. Stressing. Buying more. Eating more. Charging more.

Stressing more. More. More. And the result? Less peace. Less joy. Less perspective. Less generosity. Less conviction. And less of a sense that God is good.

Cultivating a lifestyle of contentment is simply about walking through every season with a core value of gratitude and trust and a heart that declares: *God has been good to us and He'll come through for us again. At this very moment I possess more than I can comprehend and I'm more blessed than I know. I embrace what I have today and I'll trust God for the desires of my heart. Right now, He's more than enough for me.*

When our children watch us battle through our appetites and unfulfilled desires to find contentment, they'll learn that though it's not always an easy win, it is possible, and it is a good fight. When they hear us regularly thanking God for the specific blessings in our life, they will remember that they too are blessed. When they see us giving to others more often than grabbing for ourselves, they will see—at least for us—that "stuff" is a gift and not a source.

In his somewhat cynical but boldly truthful book *Spoiled Rotten*, author Fred G. Gosman wrote this:

As we give our children more and more, we seem to be demanding and receiving less and less. Trendiness and excess are often winning the battle against respect, civility, and family unity . . .

> when our kids hear us regularly **THANKING GOD** for the specific blessings in **OUR LIFE**, they will remember that they too are **BLESSED**.

There is a marvelous saying that "there is nothing as shattering as a dream that comes true." Our children need to dream, to have things to look forward to, things to hope for. When through the best of intentions we satisfy these dreams prematurely, we are unintentionally robbing our kids of anticipation, excitement, and optimism.[3]

Giving our children what they want after they've sufficiently whined and complained to us for an hour is like feeding a monster a steak and then wondering why he repeatedly ends up on our doorstep to torment us. When our kids are in a discontented mood, the *last* thing we must do for them is to give in to their demands—unless of course, they're holding us hostage.

We must go after discontentment in our children with the same resolve we seek to uproot pride because both are rooted in a sinful, selfish mind-set—and these are not the kinds of things we want growing in our kids.

It's important to note that shedding tears because of a broken heart or a hope deferred is much different than a stomping fit. Both we and our children will endure times of heartache and weariness. Each of us at different times will wake up to days of gray skies and postponed breakthroughs. We'll be sick and tired of being sick and tired, and we'll long for the things for which we've been praying.

On such days, God doesn't breathe a heavy sigh and wave us off with a dismissing hand. On the contrary, He aches for us when we ache in this way. He has made provision for us in those waiting seasons. He is near to the brokenhearted. He wraps His arms around us when we're vulnerable and in need of some fresh courage. And He wants us to do the same for our weary kids.

But for the entitled, demanding, foot-stomping child, the only proper response is one of discipline and intervention.

Be prepared to leave the store, the restaurant, or the park. Cancel plans, interrupt conversations, and do what you have to do to take care of the outburst on the spot. Doing so sends the message to your child (and to the world): your character means so much to me that I'm willing to inconvenience myself any day of the week to deal with your wrong behaviors and misguided perspectives!

Once you've reestablished your authority in the situation and your child is on the other side of his or her tantrum (and the emotions have died down), that's the perfect time to come alongside them, love on them, and unapologetically teach them perspective in an age appropriate manner. And if his or her demanding outbursts continue, it's time to take a few of your child's luxuries and give them away to someone in need. Be relentless with this issue. It'll be worth it in the years to come.

The key to true contentment is hope. If, in times of abundance, we shift our weight (our hope) onto the things we own, and we expect those things to carry us, though we may enjoy a false sense of security for a time, ultimately those things will fail us, and our footing will be shakier than it was before. And if, during times of scarcity, we refuse contentment until we get what we want, we'll only be postponing

CONTENTMENT until we get what we want, we'll only be postponing the **TRUE JOY** that could be ours today!

if we refuse **CONTENTMENT** until we get what we want, we'll only be postponing the **TRUE JOY** that could be ours today!

the true joy that could be ours today!

We can learn to be content with much or with little when we live with open hands and a heart that trusts in God. He gives. He takes away. He's always watching out for us. And He loves us beyond words. Besides, as the old song reminds us, this world is not our home. We're just passing through.

"You're blessed when you're content with just who you are—no more, no less. That's the moment you find yourselves proud owners of everything that can't be bought. You're blessed when you've worked up a good appetite for God. He's food and drink in the best meal you'll ever eat." (Matthew 5:5–6 THE MESSAGE)

count your blessings

- If you have food in the refrigerator, clothes on your back, a roof over your head, and a place to sleep…you are richer than 70 percent of this world.

- If you have money in the bank, in your wallet, and spare change in a dish someplace…you are among the top 8 percent of the world's wealthy.

- If you woke up this morning with more health than illness…you are more blessed than the million who will not survive this week.

- If you have never experienced the danger of battle, the loneliness of imprisonment, the agony of torture, or the pangs of starvation…you are ahead of 500 million people in the world.

- If you can attend a church meeting without fear of harassment, arrest, torture, or death . . . you are more blessed than three billion people in the world.

- If your parents are still alive and still married . . . you are very rare.

- If you hold up your head with a smile on your face and are truly thankful . . . you are blessed because, although the majority can, most do not.[4]

personal application:

- Begin every day counting your blessings and thanking God. Start a thankfulness journal. Make notes in it as often as you can.

- When you notice yourself feeling discontented, retrace your steps and find out where your perspective changed. Ask God for a renewed perspective. Count your blessings once again and thank your heavenly Father.

- Regularly check up on those who have less than you and offer help whenever possible, e.g., the sick, the homeless, the hungry, the hurting. When you come home, pray for those you've just helped; count your blessings, and thank Jesus for all you have.

parental application:

- Every morning, pray with your child and together thank the Lord for specific blessings you enjoy.

- Every night, pray with your child and thank the Lord for supplying ALL of your needs.

- Every day, point out to your child the countless ways that you are truly rich. Help them to learn at a young age that every good gift comes from above (see James 1:17).

Precious Lord,

You are all that I need. Help me to cultivate a lifestyle of thanksgiving and divine perspective. Open my eyes that I may see the innumerable ways You've blessed me. Awaken my heart to care for those who have less than me. And help me to sow countless seeds of peace and content- ment into the soil of my child's heart. I love You, Lord. Amen.

Section Three

ENCOURAGE FAITH

teach forgiveness

GOD IS LOVE

If someone is caught in a sin, you who are spiritual should restore him gently. But watch yourself, or you also may be tempted.

(GALATIANS 6:1)

"Forgiveness is not an occasional act,
it is a permanent attitude."[1]

—*MARTIN LUTHER KING, JR.*

O ur firstborn, Jake, was our compliant child. He made us look good. For a while there, we actually thought we were good parents. At least that is until we had our strong-willed second son, Luke. It didn't take us long to realize that there would be no coasting in this parenting thing. Even for the compliant child, there is a fallen nature within just waiting to come out and party. Luke made us better parents to all three of our sons. He kept us on our toes and kept our discernment high.

Still, Jake was mostly easy to parent. Yes, he had his moments and his phases that made me cringe and pray more earnestly, but we always had wide-open lines of communication with him. I never wondered how Jake was doing or what he was thinking. We processed everything together. Once, he was so engrossed in sharing a story with me, he followed me to the bathroom and kept talking while I stepped into the bathroom and slowly closed the door (I had to go bad).

I peeked out at him and said, "I'm sorry, honey. I'm closing the door now. I really have to go to the bathroom." He just sucked in another breath and said, "Okay. Okay, but just one more thing." Jake continued to tell his story until I shut the door. Then he persisted and talked through the door without missing a beat. We laughed about that one later.

Jake is a connoisseur of good music. He graduated from college with a business degree with an emphasis on music business. He now works in Nashville on the business side of Christian music. One of my sweetest memories with Jake happened the summer before he left for college.

We were in the kitchen. Jake sat on the counter and talked to me about a thousand things while I emptied the dishwasher and cut up vegetables for a salad. Suddenly, he said, "Oh, Mom! You *have* to hear this song! You'll love it!" With two of my three sons being musicians, I've listened to more songs than I can count.

I followed Jake to the family room and sat down on the couch. He put on a Shane and Shane album of live worship. The music was so beautiful, so worshipful; I stretched out on the couch and embraced the moment. I closed my eyes and got lost in the lyrics. For a brief moment, I was alone with Jesus. I thanked God for such an awe-inspiring album. Then I remembered Jake.

This was my son's music. With one eye I peeked down on the floor to see Jake sprawled out on the floor with his eyes closed, thoroughly enjoying the song. I was completely moved by the idea that he was the one who initiated this pause in our day. I was also choked up at the thought of my firstborn son moving far away from home and into his next phase of life.

Without thinking, I reached down and put my hand on Jake's arm. Instantly he reached up and held my hand. He was on the floor. I was on the couch. Our eyes were closed. His hand embraced mine. I almost couldn't breathe. That moment was incredibly sacred to me.

Now lest you think Jake waltzed through his teen years without pushing the envelope, I assure you, he didn't do any waltzing, and he challenged us on plenty of occasions. He pushed and pressed for his way when it differed from ours. We consistently listened, issued an occasional compromise, and held our ground when it mattered. We also challenged his thinking on numerous occasions. We said no to certain outings, to an eyebrow ring, a lip ring, and a tattoo. We said yes to an earring (a small hoop), but that didn't bother me at all. He loved Jesus, but he went through a phase when he was drawn to a more edgy look (and that *did* bother me). We both had to search our hearts for our reasons for wanting the things we did. At the end of the day, it was all about appearances. For both of us.

One winter day, Jake asked to use my Chevy Blazer to drive to a friend's house to spend the night. He and several guys planned to get together and work on his friend's car in the garage. My husband was out of town on business and wouldn't be back for a couple of days. The weather forecasters predicted a snowstorm, and I had planned to stay home for the night.

"You can use my truck under one condition. Once you get to your friend's house, you're in for the night. No going anywhere. The roads are supposed to get really bad, and I'd have no way to get to you if something happened. Got it?" Jake smiled huge and said, "Got it! Thanks, Mom! I'll be back home in the morning in time to go to church."

The next morning I was in the bathroom blow-drying my hair when Jake walked in. His eyes were red and looked a bit swollen. I stopped the dryer and put it down. "Are you okay, honey? What's wrong?" I asked as I stepped closer to Jake. He shook his head and just said, "Oh, Mom. I'm so sorry. I'm so sorry."

My heart started beating faster, and I asked, "What? What? Tell me!" With pools of tears in his eyes and quivering lips, Jake started talking. "We were working on the car, having a great time. We'd been at it for a few hours when we got stuck and needed a part to continue. Without thinking about it, they said, 'Let's go!' and we hopped in the truck and headed to the store. Even at *that* point it didn't occur to me that I was doing anything wrong because the weather had cleared up, and I had forgotten that I had promised not to go anywhere. But then on the way home we passed by a school parking lot that was covered with a thick blanket of fresh snow.

"The guys challenged me to pull into the parking lot and do a few doughnuts. At that moment I remembered what I had promised you. I felt sick to my stomach. The guys pressed harder and said, 'Dude, don't be a girl. Just pull in and swerve around a little. It'll be fun!' They all chimed in, and so I pulled into the parking lot."

With my jaw clenched and my eyes fixed on my son, I said, "Show me the car." Together we walked out onto the snowy, unplowed driveway and took a look at my truck. The whole left side was smashed in and the side mirror hung by a cable. I shook my head, and we walked in the house. I looked up at Jake and said, "I need a minute to think through this. I need to call your dad. You stay here and deal with what you've just done to my trust and my truck!" I was furious.

> I told him how much I **LOVED** him and that we'd get through this. There would be **CONSEQUENCES**, but we'd get through it **TOGETHER**.

Long story short, the guys had swerved around, did their doughnuts, and somehow Jake slammed the truck into a concrete structure, causing no damage to the concrete but about three thousand dollars in damage to my vehicle. I couldn't believe it.

I cried. I yelled at him. I told him that I needed some time to process this whole thing. After a couple of hours the air was less hot around the house. I had spoken to Kevin, and we prayed together on the phone. We talked about how we were going to proceed. Then I went down to Jake's room and wrapped my arms around him. I told him how much I loved him and that we'd get through this. There would be consequences, but we'd get through it together.

Once I made my way upstairs, I heard Luke up in his room sobbing uncontrollably. I couldn't remember the last time he'd had a meltdown. God was doing amazing things in his life, and he was growing by leaps and bounds. I couldn't imagine what was upsetting him so. I sat on Luke's bed, rolled him over so I could see his face, and I asked him, "Honey, what's wrong?" In his passionate, emotional way he blurted out, "Oh, Mom. Don't be too hard on Jake. He didn't mean it! He's my big brother, and he's become my hero. And besides, this is more like something *I* would do. Don't you think?"

I choked back a laugh and explained that we loved Jake as much as we always had. But there would be consequences (and after all, this was too big of a deal not to get a life lesson out of it).

Once Kevin returned home from his business trip, we had a family meeting with all of the kids. We talked about what happened and let Jake express his feelings about the whole ordeal. We affirmed our great love for him. We told all three of the boys that even though Jake had blown it with the truck incident, he had made many more deposits than withdrawals in the "trust" account over the years. Kevin looked at Jake and said, "I am really bummed about the expensive choice you made this past weekend, but I want you to know that I still trust you. I really do." That statement did wonders for Jake.

Even so, at sixteen years old, Jake had a $3,000 debt to pay. He took every odd job he could to put toward the debt. He painted deck railings, mowed lawns, laid sod, and washed windows. He didn't complain about the debt, and he disassociated with the friends who left him holding the bag alone.

About $1,200 and a year later, the weight of Jake's mistake started to have a negative effect on him. He kept at the odd jobs but with a heavy heart and a measure of condemnation. He seemed to be slipping into a pit of despair and discouragement from the whole ordeal. We prayed with him, encouraged him, and told him again and again that we forgave him, treasured him, and believed in him, but he couldn't seem to get out from under the weight of his own mistake (and his debt was a glaring reminder of it).

Kevin and I knew that something needed to give. We earnestly asked God for wisdom, and He gave it to us. We had the perfect plan.

"So, what do you want to do for your birthday this year, Jake?" I gave Jake's shoulder a squeeze, hoping to see that old spark in his eye again. After thinking about it, he said, "Would it be okay if we took a few of my friends to Tanner's Steakhouse for dinner?" Tanner's steak and their cheesecake were two of his favorite things on earth. Jake also had his eye on a used guitar and, more than anything, was hoping to get that guitar for his birthday.

On the night of Jake's birthday, about ten of us sat around a rectangle table and enjoyed a wonderful steak dinner. We laughed as Jake read all of the funny birthday cards he received from his friends and his brothers. Every once in a while he looked around hoping to see a guitar-shaped gift . . . or his cheesecake, whichever came first. He was equally excited for both.

Our server came out with a beautiful dessert. Jake saw the glowing candle from across the room. With an ear-to-ear smile, the server sat the plate down in front of our son. The candle glowed and lit up Jake's face. There was a pause in the air as Jake looked down at his plate.

The dessert was drizzled with chocolate. Above and below the slice of cheesecake were two words drizzled on his plate: *Debt Forgiven.*

It took a second for his thoughts to register, and then Jake stood up so forcefully his chair almost tipped backwards. Right there in the busy restaurant, surrounded by his buddies and his family, Jake wrapped his arms around us, buried his face in our shoulders, and started to cry. I literally felt the burden lift from his shoulders.

Forgiveness took on a whole new meaning for all of us that day.

❁ ❁ ❁

Where would we be without forgiveness? How could we possibly function without the Lord's new mercies *every* morning? Looking back at our family structure now that my kids are grown, I see forgiveness as the rebar of the family. Ironically, a rebar is the steel bar that reinforces concrete. When Jake smashed up my truck, the concrete showed no evidence of the encounter.

Jake's choice from that day is a distant memory, but what we learned about the power of a debt forgiven still affects us today. As Martin Luther King Jr. so eloquently penned in the quote at the beginning of the chapter, forgiveness is a *permanent* (built-in) attitude. It's a way of life for the believer in Christ. With forgiveness in its structure, a family can withstand sins, mistakes, and missteps and come out on the other side strong, loving, and steadfast.

"God is looking for people with perfect hearts, not a perfect performance. We get a lot more concerned about our weaknesses than He does. He knows that our weaknesses are simply places where He might show Himself strong in us."[2]

Isn't it something how the family structure is meant to so beautifully portray the kingdom of God? Forgiveness and reconciliation, love and mercy, a safe place to grow and to fall down . . . these are priceless gifts from a loving Father. He lifted a mighty debt from our shoulders, one that would have crushed us, and He carried it Himself. He paid our debt with His blood. While we were yet sinners, Christ died for us (see Romans 5:8).

Obviously, forgiveness isn't a "get out of jail free" card. In fact, there are many Christians literally in jail right now for breaking the law. Has God forgiven them? If they humbled themselves and repented, yes, He forgave them. But He still allowed them to endure the consequences. Forgiveness is about reconciling a relationship. Consequences are the results of choices.

Do not be deceived: God cannot be mocked. A man reaps what he sows. (Galatians 6:7)

Forgiveness is such a costly gift that it must never be interpreted as leniency or an easy way out. We owe it to our children to walk them through the healthy process of what it means to:

• Own and admit one's offense
• Ask for forgiveness
• Take responsibility for reparations whenever possible
• Humbly embrace the grace and forgiveness Jesus offers

If we rush through this process or skip it all together, we do our children and ourselves a great disservice.

When I asked my twenty-year-old son, Jordan, what he thought this chapter should include, he said, "I think forgiveness *looks* different in every situation. Sometimes forgiveness involves quick reconciliation in relationships, other times you forgive the person, but you need to make some changes on how you approach them or relate to them. And I think consequences are really an important way for kids to learn about the impact of their choices. You have to be really involved with your children and with God to know how to handle each situation in an individual way." I don't think I could have said it better myself.

> **FORGIVENESS** *looks* **different in every SITUATION.**

> *Oh, what joy for those whose disobedience is forgiven, whose sin is put out of sight! Yes, what joy for those whose record the Lord has cleared of guilt, whose lives are lived in complete honesty!* (Psalm 32:1–2 NLT)

Part of what it means to teach forgiveness to our children is to stay closely associated with our own need for mercy and forgiveness. As we walk closely with the Lord and mature in the ways of faith, we will gain an increasing awareness of just how sinful we can be (and how merciful Jesus is). Every time God raises the bar, we see how far we fall short. And this is not a bad thing.

We are never more secure than when we are humbly aware of our need for Jesus. And the more aware we become of our capacity for sin, the more amazing it is to consider the magnitude of God's love. Through Christ, God draws us to Himself and offers forgiveness for our sins, many of which we are completely ignorant about.

He knows that in a few months we'll have a complete revelation about how racist or selfish or materialistic we are, but He doesn't wait until then to love us. He loves us today. He forgives us today. But in His seriousness about sin, He'll lead us to new places of awareness, conviction, and compassion. And when He confronts our small thinking and selfish ways, our only response can be one of humble repentance.

He is patient with us during our temporary moments of amnesia when we think we have it all together. And He gently receives us back when we remember once again how great He is and how small we are.

When our children see us engage in this living-breathing-active walk of faith—offering forgiveness and receiving it again—they will see firsthand what it means to be linked in fellowship with a mighty, involved, powerful, forgiving God. Amazing love. May we parent our children the way God has parented us.

personal application:

- Regularly pray Psalm 139:23–24 and then wait and listen. If the Lord brings anything to mind, humbly ask for forgiveness and do what He asks you to do.

- Pray daily for those you find it difficult to forgive. Every day, forgive them with your heart, your mind, and your words. One day your emotions will catch up.

- Daily receive the fresh mercies God offers you. Leave your past behind. Ask for forgiveness for today's mistakes. Trust Him for tomorrow. Think about God's love every single day.

parental application:

- Tell your children the story of Peter. He loved Jesus but was also confident in his own abilities. Then he denied even knowing Christ. He went through deep grief and repentance, and Jesus forgave him and restored him. Peter was far more powerful for Christ after he'd blown it and received forgiveness than he was before his mistake.

- Explain sin in an age appropriate way, such as this: "When you lied to me today you did two things: you disobeyed God and you broke my trust. This is how you made me feel... and this is why it's important not to lie." And then walk your child through the process of restoration.

- Model forgiveness by asking your children's forgiveness when necessary. Own and admit how you let them down. Tell them how you should have handled it. Ask for their forgiveness and ask if there is any way you can make it up to them. Pray together and then put it behind you.

Precious Lord,

Thank You for the priceless gift of forgiveness and for modeling it in such a sacrificial way. Help us never to skim over the process of repentance or restoration. May we lovingly and powerfully teach our children how to own up to their mistakes and bring them to the cross. May they learn from us what it means to walk and live and breathe in the light of Your forgiveness. May they—through us—learn to love the freedom forgiveness brings. Amen.

look deeper

GOD SEES THE HEART

Therefore, if anyone is in Christ, he is a new creation; the old has gone, the new has come! **(2 CORINTHIANS 5:17)**

"Take your human feelings, multiply them exponentially into infinity, and you will have a hint of the love of God revealed by and in Jesus Christ . . . God is loving us—you and me—this moment, just as we are and not as we should be."[1]

—*BRENNAN MANNING*

---

alk about giving up a mountain for a molehill. Our bags were packed, the flights were booked, and we were scheduled to fly to Colorado in the morning. The boys and Kevin planned on skiing and snowboarding during the day while I planned to stay back in the room to write. At night we looked forward to dinners by the fire and some fun family time. The excitement and anticipation surrounding our trip came to a screeching halt while I sat on the step and stared at my son (who stared at the spilled milk and the bits of cereal on the counter). A few drops of the milk were from Jordan, but the rest of the mess was Luke's.

"Why do I have to clean up this mess? Jordan spilled some of this milk too." For the second time, I explained, "Luke, I don't care if the whole mess came from Jordan, I asked you to clean it up. Jordan cleans up plenty of the messes around here that aren't his. I'm telling you, clean up that mess or I won't allow you to go snowboarding tomorrow."

Luke stepped back, exasperated. "You're going to make me miss snowboarding on our first day of vacation?"

I stepped in closer and said, "No. You are going to make you miss snowboarding on your first day of vacation. I'm not going to argue with you. I'm not even going to negotiate with you. If this mess isn't cleaned up in five minutes, you're staying back with me. And you'll have to find something quiet to do because I have to spend my time writing tomorrow."

I sat back down on the stair and watched the scene unfold. Luke was beside himself. He didn't want to lose this power struggle, but more than that, he didn't want to miss out on one of only three days of snowboarding. Believe it or not, he waited about three and a half minutes before he decided to clean up the mess in the kitchen. And though he complied, his attitude boiled beneath the surface. He finished on time, but with a heart that was totally in the wrong place.

After the counter was cleaned off and the dishes were in the dishwasher, Luke hopped up onto the counter, crossed his arms and set his jaw like he was furious with me. I walked over to him, rested my hands on the counter—one on each side of him—I set my jaw, stared in his eyes, and said what I needed to say:

"Luke Larson, you listen to me. You can try as you might to have that kind of attitude under this roof, but it will not fly, and you will not get away with it. I think you've noticed that we've set some pretty clear boundaries for you and your brothers. And when you stay within those boundaries you have a great life and really nice parents [okay, I was quite animated and a little crazy with energy at this point]; but when you step outside those boundaries, you're going to have a different experience altogether. We are not going to make it easy for you to ruin your life. And I want you to know, with God at my side, I have it in me to hold my ground. I've got the fight, the energy, and the persistence to win in the battle of wills. Every time. Why? *Because you are worth it to me. You are worth the fight!* Do you know that you are bursting with potential? You are going to do some really huge things in this life. I just pray they are good things. Life can go one of two ways for you, Luke. You can fight us every step of the way, in which case you'll someday have to reckon those choices with God, with your brothers, and with us. Or, you can surrender that attitude, trust that we adore you, that we have your best interest at heart, and live a life greater than you can imagine, because you'll be following God. *You* are the one who has to choose which way you'll go. But you're the one who will have to live with that choice. Just know that while you're under this roof, we are going to fight with you, if it means fighting for you, because we love you so very much."

Luke was speechless, and I was exhausted. I wrapped my arms around him, and he quietly hugged me back.

Some may wonder why I would impose such a harsh consequence for a little spilled milk and bits of cereal on the counter. I hope it's clear from the story that the mess was very much beside the point. The rebellious nature within the heart of my precious child was the battleground for which I was fighting. If left alone, that untamed will could affect every area of his life, and I couldn't let that happen.

Luke wasn't just a strong-willed boy; he was a passionate, caring soul. He was affectionate and loving and hilariously funny. But none of that would matter if he failed to see how important he was to us and to God.

Something changed in Luke's attitude after that face-off in the kitchen, and he was a pure delight on the ski trip. That incident along with an encounter with his brother were catalysts for Luke's transformation. Luke now bears no resemblance to that once strong-willed child. He loves Jesus first and foremost. He is a worship leader. He loves and fears God. He cherishes his wife. As a young, married man, he regularly calls us and humbly asks for our wisdom. He is a gentle giant, and I respect him immensely. In the worst of our struggles with Luke, God gave us eyes to see what *He* saw in that wonderful yet feisty, strong-willed boy of ours. Thank You, Lord.

❀

❀

❀

Jesus was a master at seeing the destiny in a person. The gospel of John records the first disciples who followed Jesus. Read the following passage:

When he saw Jesus passing by, he said, "Look, the Lamb of God!" When the two disciples heard him say this, they followed Jesus. Turning around, Jesus saw them following and asked, "What do you want?" They said, "Rabbi" (which means Teacher), "where are you staying?" "Come," he replied, "and you will see." So they went and saw where he was staying, and spent that day with him. It was about the tenth hour. (John 1:36–39)

I love this passage. Jesus—the One who would die for the sins of His followers—invited them to, "Come and see." He was never one for pat answers or useless clichés. Jesus wanted His disciples to learn by discovery; to grow within the context of a living, breathing relationship; and to change because they were more acquainted with His love than with their own tendencies toward sin. He invites us on the same journey. Jesus knows that we're not who we will be, but He sees what we can be, and so He invites us to follow Him, knowing that we'll be transformed along the way.

> Jesus knows that we're not WHO WE WILL BE, but He sees WHAT WE CAN BE.

Andrew, Simon Peter's brother, was one of the first men to follow Jesus. Right away he went to find his brother, Simon, to tell him, "We have found the Messiah!" Read this passage:

And he brought him to Jesus. Jesus looked at him and said, "You are Simon son of John. You will be called Cephas" (which, when translated, is Peter). (John 1:42)

I can picture Jesus narrowing His eyes just a bit, focusing in on Simon, and envisioning his God-given destiny. Underneath Peter's unrefined, hasty, impulsive nature, there was a mighty, humble man of faith. A man God would use to change the world. Jesus always looks at the heart.

Next, Jesus went to Galilee, found Philip, and invited him to become a disciple. Philip went to find Nathanael and excitedly told him, "We have found the very person the prophets wrote about! His name is Jesus, son of Joseph, from Nazareth!"

It's surprising how many disciples dropped everything on the spot and followed Jesus. Perhaps they lived with such an awareness of the living God that they were ready when His Son called them to walk alongside Him. Nathanael, though somewhat cynical, had what I think would be a more typical response to such a radical call. He said, "Nazareth! Can *anything* good come from there?" Thankfully, Philip persisted and said, "Just come and see for yourself."

Now picture the scene—Jesus knows Nathanael expressed a little attitude about the idea of this Messiah. He knows Nathanael was dragging his feet and needed a little prodding to come and meet the Savior of the world. But let's look at Jesus' response to this man:

When Jesus saw Nathanael approaching, he said of him, "Here is a true Israelite, in whom there is nothing false." "How do you know me?" Nathanael asked. Jesus answered, "I saw you while you were still under the fig tree before Philip called you." (John 1:47–48)

Jesus sees. Jesus knows. Jesus loves. And Jesus calls us, just as we are. Notice, He didn't scold Nathanael for spouting his doubts; He looked past the externals and into the heart. Jesus identified Nathanael not as the sum of his flaws but rather as a valuable soul with boundless potential.

So how do we *look deeper* that we might see what God sees in our children, especially when they behave in selfish, rude, and dis- respectful ways?

We walk with God. We pray daily and earnestly for our children. We look for ways that God is working in and all around them and, to borrow a phrase from Henry Blackaby, we join Him in that work.

In a previous chapter, I suggested that we regularly pray this prayer out of Psalm 139: "Search me, O God, and know my heart; test me and know my anxious thoughts. See if there is any offensive way in me, and lead me in the way everlasting" (Psalm 139:23–24).

As Christ-followers, Jesus calls us to regularly and prayerfully give Him access to our character that He might extract from us those things the devil would love to use against us. Jesus wants us to be more like Him so that we might live the abundant, fruitful lives for which we were created. And it's the same with our children.

As parents, it's a great idea to pray the Psalm 139 prayer *on behalf of* our children. I often prayed prayers like this one: *Lord, God, teach me to see what You see in my children. Help me to love them like You do. Point out to me anything in them that offends You and show me how to lead them in the way they should go. Give me eyes to see, ears to hear, and supernatural wisdom to know how and when to battle on their behalf. Give me the courage and the backbone and the love to parent them the way You have parented me. Amen.*

If we stay in step with the Lord and parent our kids out of *response to Him* rather than *reaction to them*, then our actions will far more

> if **WE STAY** in step with the Lord and parent our kids out of **RESPONSE TO HIM** rather than **REACTION TO THEM**, then our actions will far more likely hit **THEIR MARK**.

likely hit their mark and bring about a real change of heart rather than just an external compliance.

In the Old Testament we read a story of contrasts between the young prophet Samuel and the sons of Eli, the priest. Eli's sons were wicked, irreverent, demanding, and they blasphemed against the Lord. Samuel, on the other hand, was humble, obedient, and honorable. Samuel grew in favor with both God and man while Eli's sons grew bolder in their wicked ways. Finally, a prophet confronted Eli for the sins of his sons. The prophet asked Eli a very thought-provoking question on behalf of God Almighty:

Why do you scorn my sacrifice and offering that I prescribed for my dwelling? Why do you honor your sons more than me by fattening yourselves on the choice parts of every offering made by my people Israel? (1 Samuel 2:29)

Eli did confront his sons for their wickedness but it was too little too late. He didn't uproot the weed when it was a seed. Eli allowed his sons to grow into arrogant, demanding, spoiled men who neither feared God nor cared about people. He obviously didn't care enough about them to get a God-perspective for their lives. Instead, he allowed those boys to default to arrogance, pride, and irreverence. And God had had enough. Read what God said to Samuel about Eli's sons in 1 Samuel 3:11–14.

Look again at the prophet's question to Eli. "Why do you honor your sons more than Me?" Does this verse hit you like it hit me? Eli had honored his sons more than the Lord. There's a lesson here for all of us.

When we avoid necessary conflict with our kids, we honor them above the Lord. When we throw our hands up and allow them to listen to music or watch movies that are blatantly evil—in our own home— simply because we're tired of the battle, we honor our kids' desires (desires that will consequently ruin them) instead of honoring God.

By the way, the "Christian" opinion about what music is bad to listen to and which movies are sinful to watch ranges far and wide. Some believers feel that the only option in this day is to not own a TV and to listen only to Christian music. Other Christians feel fine about listening to general market music as long as the lyrics are okay. Some Christians feel comfortable with fast-forwarding through certain parts of an R-rated movie while others will only watch PG or PG-13 movies.

This line, this battle, is individual for each household. We are accountable before God, not to our fellow Christians who might have a standard different than ours. But even so, before God, let us look at ways we might unknowingly give more credence to our children than to God. *Blessed is the family whose God is the Lord!*

Growing grateful kids requires courage, backbone, conviction, and an honest heart before the Lord. When our kids react in ways that are disproportionate to the moment, may we press in and ask God for divine insight. May we slow down long enough to ask a few questions:

- Is there something we are missing?
- Has our son or daughter endured something that we don't know about?
- Are they feeling especially insecure?
- Is there an attitude surfacing that needs direct intervention?

Instead of quickly reacting to their reaction and telling our kids how they should feel, may we have the divine insight to slow down and ask God to help us uncover the pain or the sin beneath the surface that we might be a catalyst of healing and truth for our children.

I often liken the process to untying a knot. When our kids over-react or behave in horrible ways, there's always something awry beneath the surface. The best way to untangle the knot is to help your children retrace their "emotional steps" by asking questions about their feelings and how they perceive their lives. Often emo-tional hurts will come out of left field and you may have a few knots to untie, but if you stick with it, you'll most likely get to a place where they feel heard, understood, loved, and validated. That's the perfect time to reset the standard of the home and reaffirm your child's amazing value to both God and you.

Almost twenty years ago, I heard Dr. Gary Smalley give a profound piece of advice to parents. He said (my paraphrase here), "Never let your child walk away with a closed spirit. Always make sure you work through the issue to the point where you see them open up to you again. If you leave their spirit closed, their heart will eventually grow cold and you'll lose the opportunity to speak into their lives and lead them in the way they should go."

I never forgot that advice. Our children have the potential of being tomorrow's leaders. They are tomorrow's business owners, attorneys, pastors, wives, husbands, fathers, mothers, elders, and neighbors. With God's help, may we be bold and insightful enough to see the Lord's image in our children. May we discern the Lord's call on our kids' lives at an early age and then cooperate with Him by making the way clear for them. And may our walk of faith be so real and so vibrant that our children will grow up to be grateful adults because they lived in a home where God was honored above everything else.

> "Always make sure you **WORK THROUGH** the issue to the point where you see them **OPEN UP TO YOU** again. If you leave their spirit **CLOSED,** their heart will eventually **GROW COLD."**

The Lord does not look at the things man looks at. Man looks at the outward appearance, but the Lord looks at the heart. (1 Samuel 16:7)

personal application:

• When you overreact or experience an emotion that seems disproportionate to the moment, get alone with God and remind yourself how much He loves you. Ask Him for wisdom to "unravel the knot" and find peace again.

• When you are tempted to judge someone else by outward appearance, ask God to give you eyes to see that person the way He does. Ask the Lord how you can best serve HIM.

• When you are tempted to do something for appearance's sake, get alone with God and ask Him to show you where your thinking is off.

parental application:

• Regularly pray and ask God what He is up to in your kids' lives. Ask Him to show you how you can cooperate with Him. Don't be satisfied with just outward compliance. Ask the Lord for insight regarding the attitude of their hearts.

• Regularly paint a "down the road" picture for your kids. In other words, show them where their "now" choices and attitudes will lead if left to go down that road. Help them to want God's best for them by explaining your reasons for your standards.

• When your child puts too much value on outward appearances, take some time and read the stories of David, Samuel, or Joseph of the Old Testament. Read contemporary stories of those who rose from obscurity to greatness. Regularly tell your kids about all of the significant things you "see" in them. Speak to them often about their potential and of God's greatness within them.

Precious Lord,

Thank You for loving me as I am and for loving me too much to leave me that way. Help me to have eyes to see things as You do. Grant me heightened discernment so I can love and guide my kids from a heavenly perspective. Grow them into godly, wonderful human beings, Lord! Give me faith to believe that You are doing great things in them and me. I don't want to get lost in the moment. I want to live my life and parent my children as someone who is loved by almighty God and who has constant and continual access to His presence. Because I am and I do. Thank You, Lord. Amen.

pray boldly

GOD LOVES FAITH

"Ask and it will be given to you; seek and you will find; knock and the door will be opened to you. For everyone who asks receives; he who seeks finds; and to him who knocks, the door will be opened."

(MATTHEW 7:7–8)

"Everything depends on our relationship to the name; the power it has on my life is the power it will have in my prayers."[1]

—ANDREW MURRAY

One night, when our kids were still quite young, I sat on the edge of Jake's bed and listened in amazement as he prayed a passionate prayer: "I thank You, God, for my new bunk beds and my dinosaur bedspread and my bright new walls and my cool new poster. I love them so much." He squeezed his eyes shut as he prayed.

My eyes were wide open. I looked around at the beige walls in deep need of paint. I glanced down at his old, worn bed and bedspread. Both were hand-me-downs. No posters decorated the walls;

no dinosaurs brought life to his room. This was a tough time for us, and, though I knew of Jake's deep desire for a fresh, new bedroom, I couldn't even imagine providing one for him.

But our situation didn't seem to affect our son's prayers one single bit.

Jacob saw the sad question on my face and yet confidently replied, "It's okay, Mom. I just know that I'm going to love those things when I get them, so I decided to get a head start on thanking God."

"Which of you, if his son asks for bread, will give him a stone? Or if he asks for a fish, will give him a snake? If you, then, though you are evil, know how to give good gifts to your children, how much more will your Father in heaven give good gifts to those who ask him!" (Matthew 7:9–11)

Our bills exceeded our income. We couldn't provide these things for our son. But in this situation, I had overlooked the fact that faith pleases God. And He can do anything He pleases. I leaned over and kissed my son's forehead and thanked Jesus with him. I agreed that nothing was too difficult for God and that He loves to give good gifts to His children. We both got a head start on thanking God for Jake's new bedroom. Praying with Jake about the desires of his heart added a fresh expectancy to our days.

Faith engages the Father's heart and compels Him to act on our behalf. He's no respecter of "persons," but He is a respecter

> **FAITH** engages the **FATHER'S HEART** and compels Him to act on **OUR BEHALF.**

of faith. My son's unrelenting faith actually engaged *my* heart and my senses as well. I looked for deals. I listened for God's direction. I reached for His provision. In no time, we stumbled upon a sale here and a sale there.

We found matching dinosaur bedspreads and sheets; we found paint we could afford; and friends gave us a great deal on a nice set of bunk beds. Within a year, Jake had bunk beds with a dinosaur bedspread. The room was transformed with a fresh coat of white and bright green accent paint. The walls came alive with cute cartoon posters.

Each night when I tucked the boys in bed, I was reminded afresh of how faith pleases God. And of how much He loves to give good gifts to His children.

Now faith is being sure of what we hope for and certain of what we do not see. (Hebrews 11:1)

Some of the greatest blessings I enjoy today are the result of earnest prayers I prayed in days past. The more I studied Scripture the more I learned that faith matters to God. Now I'm convinced that the truly righteous live by faith. God loves it when His children believe Him. We cannot please Him without faith. As I'm sure is true for you, God has shown up in our lives in ways too many to count. Please allow me to share just a few of the highlights with you now.

I came into my marriage with a very active devotional and prayer life. We had our children right away. God blessed us with three sons in four years. And though my quiver was full, my prayer life turned upside down. Sleepless nights and sick babies took the place of peaceful moments in prayer. I loved and cherished my children, but I was desperate to recapture the active devotional life I once enjoyed.

As a young mom of three little ones very close in age, I offered God my little morsel of time and asked Him to miraculously multiply it so that I could spend even more time with Him. I trusted that this was His will for me too, so I persisted in my request. I knew Jesus wanted time with me as much as I wanted time with Him. My faith grew bolder with every prayer. Eventually, I started to thank God (by faith) for a daily, thriving, devotional life (especially on the days when the idea of such a thing seemed completely impossible).

Now, many years later, my morning appointment with God has expanded in richness, depth, and duration. Every morning I get to spend a significant amount of time in prayer, study, and reflection. God took my little offering of time as a young mom, established it, and multiplied it to meet my need in each stage of my life. It's not hard for me to spend extended time with Jesus; it is, by far, the sweetest part of my day.

Through prayer God sustained our family during months of high-risk pregnancies, bed rest, and babies in the hospital. Due to the prayers of friends and family, God put me on my feet again after a terrible battle with Lyme disease. Through earnest prayer, the Lord sustained my husband on his sick bed and provided him with a new job after his battle with cancer. Kevin's job fits him perfectly and allows him room to spread his wings. He's still there today and thriving.

Probably the greatest answer to prayer for us as a family came as a result of my son Jordan's faithful, persistent prayer. I tell the full story in my book *Embracing Your Freedom: A Personal Experience in God's Heart for Justice.* That story is worth the whole price of the book if I do say so myself. In a nutshell, Jordan took a late hit in football and sustained a serious back injury when he was only seventeen years old. He went six months shuffling through life, only able to lift his leg a few inches off the floor. His world shrank along with his atrophying muscles. It was devastating to watch. We tried everything short of major back surgery. After looking at the MRI report, one doctor asked us if Jordan had lost control of his bowels yet. Thankfully, he hadn't.

We prayed every day. We thanked God by faith for a miracle. And every day, Jordan shuffled through life. But one day while at youth group, Jordan received prayer from another student and was miraculously healed! Just like that! We cried together, we thanked God together, and we are still in awe today that God allowed us to be part of such a significant, indisputable miracle.

One day not too long after he was healed, Jordan came home from football practice full of energy and spirit, still laughing from something that happened in the hallway at school. "So, Mom, one of the guys jumped in the air and tried to touch the ceiling. He couldn't do it, but the rest of us decided to give it a try. One by one we took turns at our vertical jump, and a bunch of us reached the ceiling. But then Eyo jumped so high that he pushed the ceiling tile out of place."

"What did you do?" I asked.

With a big smile on his face he said, "I got down on all fours and let Mulrooney stand on my back to put the tile back where it belonged." I literally gasped at the thought of a two-hundred-pound football player standing on my son's back while he was down on all fours. I had just spent the past six months carrying Jordan's back-pack, driving him from one doctor to another, and crying out to God to heal him.

Jordan read my mind and said right away, "Mom, I know what you're thinking, but my back is fine. Remember, God healed me! I have the strongest back on the team!" Even today I get choked up at the thought of Jordan's miracle.

Now, does that mean that everyone who prays in faith gets healed? And if someone doesn't get healed, is it because they are lacking faith? No. Not necessarily. While I do believe we would see many more miracles were there more faith on the earth, I also must say that I don't fully understand the ways of God. Some people are relentless in their faith, while day after day they watch a loved one suffer unbearably. Two of my mentors from the past died of cancer. Both were women of amazing faith. Both wanted to live, but they trusted God's ultimate purposes more. Both lived godly, fruitful lives. Both are in heaven with Jesus now. We must err on the side of faith, but then ultimately the Lord gets to decide when to take someone home.

I've been praying for a long time for my own healing. I deal daily with some significant health issues. I consistently, persistently ask God to restore my health, but in the meantime, I celebrate all of the victo-ries we've enjoyed. I cherish the countless ways God has come through for us. And I continue to believe Him for great things in the future.

And one more caveat: does praying boldly mean that we join the "bless me" club where we expect God to be our Santa Claus in the sky? Absolutely not! He is God, and we are not! But you only have to skim the Scriptures to find evidence of our call to pray. And pray boldly. The Bible tells us to pray about everything, ask for what we need, exercise our faith, and believe God will come through for us. Read through the gospels and notice how, almost more than anything else, faith made Jesus stop in His tracks and take notice. Faith is a big deal to God.

Cultivating a lifestyle of prayer is the most important legacy we can leave our children. We can tell them that they have instant access to almighty God. However, if we don't model those daily conversations, our children will consider prayer a side note in life, or a default response in hard times.

For us as Christ-followers, prayer is our oxygen. Teaching our kids to breathe in the fresh life that God offers each day, and to breathe out their worries and concerns, equips them to have a faith of their own. One of our greatest responsibilities as parents is to teach our kids to walk with Jesus as if it's the most natural thing on earth.

A.W. Tozer wrote this:

God wills that we should push on into His presence and live our whole life there. This is to be known to us in conscious experience. It is more than a doctrine to be held; it is a life to be enjoyed every moment of the day.[2]

"Prayer can do anything that God can do."[3]
—*E.M. Bounds*

From when my kids were young, I prayed with them before they walked out the door. One of the bold statements of faith they heard me pray every single day was this one: "I thank You, by faith, Lord, that NO seed of rebellion exists in Jake (or Luke, or Jordan). I thank You, Lord that he is honorable, humble, and respectful. He loves You, loves his family, and honors authority. Thank You for this mighty man of faith. Help us to parent him in a way that cooperates with Your plan for his life." And then I'd go on to pray about the specifics of each boy's day.

One morning when I was praying for my kids before they headed off to school, I heard the Lord's whisper across my heart, *pray more boldly*. So I stepped up my prayers on the spot: "I thank You, Lord that my sons love Your presence and Your Word. I thank You that You've called them to be strong and steadfast in their faith! I thank You that they are not easily deceived! They know the truth and they walk in the truth. You are going to do mighty things in and through these young men! Thank You, Lord! Amen."

One day a mom asked me, "So, do you *have* to pray out loud for your kids?" Of course, you don't have to do anything you don't want to, but the Bible does say that faith comes from *hearing* the Word of God (see Romans 10:17). With all my heart, I know that when our kids hear us praying for them with bold assurance, it does something for their own faith. It was never odd for my kids to hear us ask God for big breakthroughs on their behalf. Perhaps because that's all they ever knew.

More often than not, we tried to pray from above our circumstances rather than below them. In other words, instead of begging and pleading and hoping, we thanked God for already knowing and caring and loving. For instance, during a relational difficulty with Jake and some of his friends we prayed with him, "Lord, God, You are faithful and You will work everything together for the good [see Romans 8:28]. You love Jake, and You love his friends. We believe that You are up to something here. We will look for You in this situation, and we know that we will find You. Thanks for loving Jake so very much that You are going to do great things in this difficult situation. Amen."

It made all the difference in our prayers.

Once we are convinced that prayer actually changes things, we will make it a necessary and normal part of our day. And when our kids see us praying on the phone with a friend, or remembering a hurting family during dinner prayers, or praying in the car on the way to school, they will understand that we serve an active, involved, heavenly Father.

To remind ourselves of God's faithfulness, we need to make note of the answers to our prayers. Keep a daily prayer journal to see how God meets the needs we have laid before Him in prayer. To celebrate a long awaited breakthrough, make a special dessert. Put out the nice dishes if you have them and light a few candles. Tell the kids,

> I know that when **OUR KIDS** hear us praying for them with **BOLD ASSURANCE,** it does something for their **OWN FAITH.**

"We are celebrating the special goodness of God tonight!"

> *Do not be anxious about anything, but in everything, by prayer and petition, with thanksgiving, present your requests to God. And the peace of God, which transcends all understanding, will guard your hearts and your minds in Christ Jesus.* (Philippians 4:6–7)

I love the last part of that verse. His peace will guard our hearts and minds as we *live in Christ Jesus*. Part of what it means to live in Christ is to help our kids understand that anything is possible for those who believe (see Mark 9:23). How many parents make the mistake of telling their children, "That'll never happen!" or "You're not a good enough athlete to achieve that; I'm just trying to help you be realistic."

Those kinds of statements always sadden me. When we look at the motley crew that Jesus chose to change the world, and when we consider the idea that He chooses the foolish to shame the wise, then we have to conclude that Jesus doesn't call the qualified; He qualifies those who are brave enough to respond to His call.

Instead of painting dreary, realistic scenarios for our kids, how about if we impart faith and vision and conviction that they might go on and change the world? And what about truth-telling? How do we balance these lofty visions with the reality of their weak-

> Instead of painting **DREARY,** realistic scenarios for our kids, how about if we impart **FAITH** and **VISION** and **CONVICTION** that they might go on and change the **WORLD?**

nesses? We'll address that issue in the next chapter, but for now, may we be inspired to pray boldly—out loud so our kids can hear us—for our world, our family, and our children's future.

In his fabulous book *Beyond Jabez*, author Bruce Wilkinson wrote:

God wants very much to work in our lives, on earth, far more than we want Him to work in our lives! He constantly scans, east to west, north to south, seeking loyal hearts. Why? In order to show Himself strong by working in our lives. You can rest assured that it's God's desire to release His hand of power. And you can be confident that He wants to do it through you. Are you ready?[4]

"When the Son of Man comes, will he find faith on the earth?" (Luke 18:8)

personal application:

- Practice praying Scripture out loud, every day. Here are a few verses to get you started: Psalm 139:5; Mark 11:22–24; Philippians 4:13, 19; Ephesians 3:20.
- Add faith to your prayers. Picture your words igniting activity in heaven. Prayer changes things.
- Start a prayer journal and record the answers when they come. Share those breakthroughs with family and friends (faith comes from hearing).

parental application:

- Pray bold prayers with your children every morning and every night. Ask God to show you how to pray specifically for each one. He'll lead the way.

- Ask your kids to pray their own prayers of faith. They'll grow into this.

- Encourage your children to exercise faith on a regular basis. Don't hesitate to ask them on occasion, "So, what are you believing God for these days?" Just as our bodies need regular exercise, so does our faith.

Precious Lord,

Thank You for inviting us to dialogue with You. Thank You for making a way for me to come into Your presence and enjoy Your promises. Help me never to take such a gift for granted. Stir up my faith and awaken me to the many ways You are working around me. Help me to impart fresh faith into my children that they may have an active and real prayer life. May You be pleased by the faith in our family. Amen.

speak the truth

GOD HONORS INTEGRITY

God wants us to grow up, to know the whole truth and tell it in love—like Christ in everything. We take our lead from Christ, who is the source of everything we do. **(EPHESIANS 4:15 THE MESSAGE)**

"To teach is to learn twice."[1]

—JOSEPH JOUBERT

During a family meeting one night, my twelve-year-old son Luke leaned forward and shared this observation with me: "The other night when you had those women over for dinner, I heard a couple of them swear. Now I know your heart is sad because a couple of your friendships recently fell apart, but I think you have to be especially careful about who you replace those friends with. Maybe this isn't the time to find new friends. Maybe this is a time to figure out why those other friendships fell apart."

I felt thoroughly confronted and somewhat embarrassed by my son's sincere, yet adult-like confrontation. The truth is, the dinner party to which he referred was actually a work meeting. I was an aerobics coordinator, and my guests were also aerobics coordinators for the same club system. Ours was a dinner meeting, and though these women were not crude, I suppose a couple of them used a choice word or two.

And regarding my failed friendships, he was right. I had just come through a couple of excruciating conflicts, and my heart was still broken from the pain of it all. I was in a vulnerable place and I *did* need to be careful. Even so, it was difficult to be corrected by an adolescent boy. But we were the ones who had set the stage for such a thing.

From the start, we wanted our kids accustomed to hearing straight talk—in love, of course, but without hidden messages or implied meanings. Every couple of months we had family meetings where we reestablished the family ground rules, especially if we were heading into a new season:

• Christmastime is not about me
• Summertime does not make mom the maid
• The school season calls for more structure

We also used these meetings as a time to dig a little deeper in our relationships with one another. We really wanted our kids to know how to lovingly and confidently give and receive correction. We thought that if, from a young age and within a controlled atmosphere, they got used to hearing about their strengths and their growth areas, then it wouldn't feel like an indictment when their teacher or their future boss or spouse confronted them.

We knew we'd be giving our sons (and those in relationship with them) a great gift if we could teach them how to separate their value (already established in Christ) with their character (always developing until we see Jesus). Francis Frangipane once said, "We cannot grow beyond our ability to receive correction."

So as a regular component to our family meetings, we took some time for each of us to share what we observed to be a strength and a growth area for each member of the family. We set some ground rules first:

- Be respectful and loving
- Give an example
- Be encouraging
- Be willing to forgive
- Listen and don't respond until the other person is finished

This wasn't easy to do, and sometimes it took us awhile to untie some of the knots that were before us.

At one particular meeting, little Jordan leaned into my shoulder and hid part of his face. Then his lips started to quiver as he spoke to Jake. "You are so nice to me, and you always share things with me [strength], but when your friends are around . . ." Jordan started to cry, but continued, ". . . it seems like you don't even care about me anymore. Like I'm invisible!"

Jake waited to make sure Jordan was finished before he responded. He nodded and then said, "You're right, JoJo, I *do* do that. When I have my friends over, I don't really think about how that makes you feel, but I'll try to pay attention to that from now on. I'm sorry, bud."

At different times the boys told Kevin how much they appreciated his kindness and his patience, but they wished he wouldn't work so much. On occasion the boys told me that though they loved how much I loved them, they wished I wouldn't worry so much.

We noticed that though Jake was nice to everyone, he wasn't always careful in his associations. And though Luke was careful not to overcommit to things, he was sometimes selfish with his time. And though Jordan was extremely kind and wouldn't hurt a flea, he repeatedly left a messy trail throughout the house.

These meetings were rarely easy and always humbling. I guess it takes some effort to dig beneath the surface, but that's where peace is found.

We always closed these meetings with prayer, all five of us. Not only did our sons learn a great skill in communication, they walked away from those meetings with a clean slate with their brothers and with us. They knew they would regularly have the chance to say the hard thing within a safe context and it did wonders for our relationships.

Whoever loves discipline loves knowledge, but he who hates correction is stupid. Reckless words pierce like a sword, but the tongue of the wise brings healing. (Proverbs 12:1, 18)

Speaking the truth when the truth is unpleasant is, well, just that: unpleasant. Difficult things are easier left unsaid. But relationships are only as safe as they are true. God wants us to navigate through our relationships with conviction, integrity, and love, especially within the family.

All too often we prefer to avoid conflict, and we thus default to a surface level of peace, which isn't really peace at all. "Surface peace" is just the absence of waves or conflict. To me, avoiding a necessary confrontation is like refusing to throw up when you have the flu. You won't look messy, but you'll feel miserable.

So how do we cultivate a peaceful home with truth as a centerpiece? Often we think that peace is defined by how things appear. If a family appears not to have any conflict, we may think they have it all together. But this is not always the case.

> there is a big difference between the "PEACEKEEPER" and the "PEACEMAKER."

There is a big difference between the "peacekeeper" and the "peacemaker." The peacekeeper works tirelessly to avoid conflict in order to preserve the appearance that "all is well; no conflict here," all the while sweeping hard feelings and unresolved issues under the rug.

Peacekeeping family systems are often marked by passivity or even passive-aggressive tendencies. On the surface they may be sweet and meek, but underneath they can be stubborn and manipulative. Telling the truth in a simple and sincere manner seems too difficult, so they may hide a message inside their humor. Peacekeepers also tend to endure circumstances well past their "grace limit" and finally end up blowing a gasket when no one sees it coming.

Peacemakers, on the other hand, are determined to have true inner peace and will therefore live from the truth and deal openly and honestly with conflict. Which means, they will have conflict on occasion.

James 3:17–18 says, "But the wisdom that comes from heaven is first of all pure; then peace-loving, considerate, submissive, full of mercy and good fruit, impartial and sincere. Peacemakers who sow in peace raise a harvest of righteousness." Note that *sowing* requires digging beneath the surface.

Though it takes hard work and a commitment to truth and integrity, there is something powerful about thoughtfully listening, humbly apologizing, and lovingly choosing to live in peace with those around you.

The family at peace regularly:

• Guards against weeds of bitterness and unforgiveness
• Takes care of the little things before they become big things
• Makes regular deposits in every other family member
• Gives the children a chance to teach and to be taught

We give our children a great gift when we teach them how to lovingly handle the truth, walk in the truth, and embrace the freedom the truth brings. On a practical level, the truth may sound like this:

"I do love your picture, honey. I don't think it's your best work, but it's very nice."

Or, "You looked really tired out there tonight. Are you feeling okay? I appreciated how you hustled, but you didn't have your usual steam."

Or, "I so appreciate how you've been picking up after yourself around here; that means a lot to me. But even more important to me is how you treat your brothers and sisters. I'm not sure why you think it's okay to treat them like that, but it's not. They have as much of a right to live under this roof as you do, and you need to look at what lie you're believing that makes you think you're more special than they are. This is a serious issue, and we need to get to the bottom of it. You have it in you to be a great big brother!"

Or, "Honey, you have a tendency to be a tattletale. You point out other's flaws far more than you look at yourself, and that's a bad habit to get into. Of course, I want to know about it if someone is doing something dangerous, but if you're tempted to run and tell about every little thing, ask Jesus to show you what He wants to change in you first. Let's talk and pray about that."

"He who listens to a life-giving rebuke will be at home among the wise." (Proverbs 15:31)

Both Kevin and I have met far too many adults who were not teachable or even open to constructive criticism. They completely shut down at the thought of confrontation. They were highly functional in one area of life and completely immature in another. Early on, we saw how crippling that kind of insecurity could be and didn't want that for our sons.

As someone who was painfully insecure in my younger days, it took me years and lots of inner healing to learn how freeing the truth can be. But once I learned first and foremost that nothing could ever separate me from God's love, and that He disciplines those He loves, I wanted God to have full access to my character.

The problem I ran into later in life was that in my zeal to be everything God intended me to be, I gave everyone and anyone permission to tell me what they thought of me. Sadly, that opened the door to all kinds of petty and mean comments. Through a loving and cautionary word from a friend, I learned that it was wise to have healthy boundaries and to be selective about whose "painful truth" statements I allowed to affect me.

And there lies the rub with telling the truth in love. We must discern when it's our duty to speak a difficult word to someone we love and when it's our place to step back and pray about what we see. Timing and discernment are foundational when it comes to saying the difficult word, especially to our children.

Furthermore, we must be so secure in who we are in Christ that when others speak words to us that clearly do not reflect God's heart or tone, we know how to process their words in a way that doesn't devastate us. To have integrity in our words, boundaries around our heart, and the humility to receive a God-given correction is to be someone who others respect and who

> We must **DISCERN** when it's our duty to speak a **DIFFICULT** word to someone we love and when it's our place to **STEP BACK** and **PRAY** about what we see.

God can greatly use.

This is such an important lesson for our kids. If they can understand this at an early age, they will be miles ahead of most of us when they reach adulthood. As you can probably already tell, Luke *loved* to tell the truth. He had this way of dropping a bomb in a gentle, respectful way so that the poor person didn't know what hit him. We had some work to do with that young one.

One day, when Luke was about five years old, he was lying on the floor and working on a puzzle. The doorbell rang, and Kevin hopped up and whisked by Luke to answer the door. In the process Kevin's foot bumped Luke's elbow, which made Luke's own knuckles barely bump his own face. I saw it. I was there. It was nothing.

My sweet husband was out on the doorstep talking to a complete stranger when Luke came down, patiently waited, and then raised his hand as if to say he had a question. Kevin looked down and said, "Yes, Luke." Luke calmly looked up at his papa and said, "Um, Dad. I just want you to know that I forgive you for kicking me in the head just now." What's a guy supposed to do with that?

Luke always seemed to "pronounce truth" at unexpected times. Weeks before we moved into our new house we visited the site to look at the progress. When the neighbor came over and greeted us, she asked us if we had any questions. Luke raised his hand (I held my breath), and then he asked in his calm and respectful way, "Yes, I have a question. I was wondering if you are going to do anything about that barking dog before we move in. He barks every second."

Yes, he got in trouble for that one.

In about fifth grade, Luke had a difficult teacher who happened to be enduring a terrible day. She sat at her desk, looked down, and clearly didn't know what to do. Luke apparently walked up to her, put his arm around her, and gently said, "I'm sorry you're having a bad day. Maybe it would go better for you in this class if you weren't so hard on the boys all of the time." Hmmmm.

Needless to say, we don't have to say everything that's true. We just have to make sure everything we say is true. How do we know that now is the time to bring a difficult word and if we're the one to do so?

If our confrontation comes from a self-righteous place or a let me at 'em attitude, then we are most definitely not the person to bring the corrective word. God loves that person far too much to send them a Pharisee or a person with a loaded gun.

Furthermore, if we've waited too long to bring the correction and we've built a case out of our long list of offenses, we are not the person to bring the confrontation. That account is our burden to bear and we must bring it to the cross, pray fervently for God's forgiveness for failing to obey in a timely manner, and then pray God's blessing and mercy on the one who is the object of our judgment.

On the other hand, if talking with this person is the last thing on earth we want to do, but we know we must, then, more likely than not, we are the one to bring correction. If we care so much about this person that we feel they may go off track if we don't have this uncomfortable conversation, then we are definitely the one to bring a truthful, loving word.

What does this have to do with parenting, let alone growing grateful kids? Everything, if you believe that we cannot impart something we don't possess. We have to live the truth before we can teach our kids to walk in it. And regarding our difficult conversations with them, the same ground rules apply. When we are angry and feeling especially critical is not the time to bring correction. Everyone needs a time out sometime.

There's a big difference between recklessly spewing the words, "You are so lazy," and having the restraint and wisdom to wait until you can gently but firmly say something like, "Honey, it seems you work hard not to have to work hard. Life is work and a good work ethic is essential. The Bible says that a lazy person is as bad as someone who destroys things (see Proverbs 18:9). You have too much potential to throw away all of the gifts God has given you just because you want to take the easy way out. I won't let you do that while you live under this roof because I believe in you far too much for that!"

The following verse serves as a great standard for all of us: "For your love is ever before me, and I walk continually in your truth" (Psalm 26:3).

The first part of the verse charges us to keep God's love ever before us. The second part of the verse calls us to walk continually in His truth. We keep our eyes upward on God's love, and we keep our feet on the ground, the solid ground of God's Word. God's love must be the filter through which we process information, and we must dare to ask ourselves, *Are my thoughts and observations born out of God's love for me and for others? Or*

> The so-called truth without **GOD'S LOVE** ceases to be the **ABSOLUTE TRUTH.** Without God's love, all else is **NOISE.**

are they coming out of my own cynicism, suspicion, or momentary impatience?

The so-called truth without God's love ceases to be the absolute truth. Without God's love, all else is noise. His love is what saves us, defines us, leads us, and guides us. His love redeems every sinful tendency. His love fuels us and, as long as His love serves as our filter, we will easily discern the high road in every situation. With His love before us, and His truth beneath us, we can do all things—even parent amazing children—because Christ is working mightily within us.

He who ignores discipline comes to poverty and shame, but whoever heeds correction is honored. (Proverbs 13:18)

Though Luke said some funny and inappropriate things during his formative years, I must say his gentleness and timing have become some of his greatest gifts. People come to him for advice because they know he'll offer keen insight and gentle but direct truth. He's not afraid to bring the difficult word, but he now knows how to hold his peace unless God asks him to speak up.

He said some great things to us when he graduated from high school: "Mom, Dad, I'm so thankful that you taught me how to receive correction and weren't afraid to hold your ground when I was being difficult. It doesn't even occur to me to take it personally when a teacher or a boss corrects me now. I know who I am. But I also know that I have a lot to learn, so it's okay if they have to correct me. And even though I know I was a handful growing up, you never made me feel like a problem child. You somehow made me feel like I could accomplish anything I wanted to as long as I was willing to follow Jesus and do what He says." Thank You, Lord.

Sowing peacemaking seeds into the soil of our kids' character won't exactly make them grateful right away. In fact, they may not like it very much. But when given time to grow (the child and the seed), our kids will come to love and appreciate the value of a truthful word spoken in love. In fact, they'll be miles ahead of most of their peers because so few today are willing to receive correction and humbly rise up to the occasions before them. When our kids become adults and find themselves to be confident people and competent communicators, they will be truly grateful.

May we allow God's truth to penetrate our lives in such a way that we live and breathe with love, integrity, conviction, and courage. May we teach our children how to humbly receive correction that they may grow into everything God intended them to be. And may God's peace fill our home because we live there with honest hearts.

Therefore, as God's chosen people, holy and dearly loved, clothe yourselves with compassion, kindness, humility, gentleness and patience. Bear with each other and forgive whatever grievances you may have against one another. Forgive as the Lord forgave you. And over all these virtues put on love, which binds them all together in perfect unity. Let the peace of Christ rule in your hearts, since as members of one body you were called to peace. And be thankful. (Colossians 3:12–15)

personal application:

- Pick a number of verses (like Psalm 26:3; Proverbs 31:26; and Psalm 19:14) and pray them every single day. Immerse yourself in the truth of God's word (and His desire for you to be His mouthpiece).

- Ask the Lord for a heightened sensitivity to the Holy Spirit's prompting. Ask for increased courage to bring a word of truth when it's needed.

- Give a trusted, godly friend permission to speak the truth to you. Hold each other accountable with regards to habits, time management, relationships, words, and so on.

parental application:

- Once the kids are in elementary school, make time for occasional family meetings. It's better to schedule these meetings according to need (changing seasons or changing attitudes) rather than on a fixed monthly schedule. If you're too rigid on this point, these gatherings will become a drudgery.

- If you have a younger child still in preschool or kindergarten, have them sit in on these meetings and give them a chance to talk. They'll learn by watching.

- Ask the Lord to show you how and when to speak the truth to your children, that you may train them in the way they should go (see Proverbs 22:6).

speak the truth

Heavenly Father,

You are the way, the truth, and the life! Help me to live in a way that clearly represents the beautiful truth about who You are. Open my mouth with skillful and godly wisdom and help me to live by the law of kindness. Give me insight into Your word and clarity in every situation. Help me to know when to speak, when to pray, and how to receive the correction that comes from You. I know that You only discipline those You love, and I know that You love me. Help me to convey that same kind of godly love to my children today. Amen.

Section Four

LIVE ABUNDANTLY

give a blessing

GOD IS GENEROUS

*The Lord bless you and keep you; the Lord make his face
shine upon you and be gracious to you; the Lord turn his face
toward you and give you peace.* **(NUMBERS 6:24–26)**

"'What part of God's dream is linked to your destiny?'"[1]

—BRUCE WILKINSON

We have a favorite family tradition. Every eve-of-Christmas Eve, we sit down for dinner by candlelight. As the afternoon turns to evening, the daylight is replaced by the glow of the fireplace, the lights on the Christmas tree, and the flickering candles at the dinner table.

Five Christmas china plates sit on five gold chargers. Wine glasses sit on small saucer plates. Ice water glasses sparkle in the candlelight. A cluster of warm rolls just out of the oven sits nestled in a basket on the edge of the table. The salads look festive all sprinkled with cranberries. The scent of marinated petite sirloins cooked just right lets everyone know that it's time to gather around the table. We look forward to this night every single year.

On the eve-of-Christmas Eve, we stop the hustle-bustle of the season, and we sit down to remember together and to dream together. This is a time for each of us to share three things:

- What God has done in our lives over the past year
- What we've learned
- What we want to take with us into the coming year

Then we share what we *want from the Lord* in the upcoming year. For example, one year Jake said, "I want to know, on a greater level, just what I possess in Christ. And then I want to appropriate it in my life in a more intentional manner."

But we don't start with the sharing. We pour the sparkling cider or Catawba juice, enjoy the meal, and listen to our sons banter back and forth. We laugh a lot. And when the clinking of the dishes settles down, we settle in. We let the candles burn because we know we'll be at the table for a while yet. After someone is done sharing, the rest of us take a moment to bless and affirm him or her with our own observations. No "growth areas" to talk about tonight. Only blessings. We all know it, and we love every minute of it.

This past year I learned about a tradition that the Jewish people practiced for many years on the Sabbath. Some still do. During the Sabbath meal, the father stands behind his son or daughter and places his hands on his or her shoulders. And he speaks a blessing over the child while the mother pours the wine into the glass.

The reason you need the saucer under the wine glass is because you are supposed to pour the wine (or the sparkling cider in our case) until the cup overflows, symbolizing God's blessings, which cannot be contained.[2]

This past year, Kevin and I spent the week prior to our eve-of-Eve dinner asking God for a blessing to give to each of our sons. We wanted to rightly represent Him and to speak the very words He was speaking over them in heaven. If you've never asked God for a specific blessing for your child, I encourage you to do so. God will show you His heart for your son or your daughter, and you'll be blessed in the process.

We didn't tell our boys about the new tradition until they came to the table. "We're not going to pour the Catawba just yet. We have a plan for the end of the dinner." We went on to enjoy a wonderful meal. Finally, when it was time, Kevin and I got up from the table. I picked up the bottle of Catawba and Kevin put his firm hands on our firstborn son's shoulders. I poured the sparkling cider as Kevin poured out a blessing on Jake.

The three of us choked up as we watched the purple liquid spill over the edges of Jake's beautiful glass and gather on the saucer below. What a perfect way to illustrate how God fills our cup to overflowing. One by one we moved around the table, blessed our sons, and filled their cups until they spilled over.

You prepare a table before me in the presence of my enemies. You anoint my head with oil; my cup overflows. Surely goodness and love will follow me all the days of my life, and I will dwell in the house of the Lord forever. (Psalm 23:5–6)

Just yesterday while I was listening to Don Moen's radio show, I heard one of his guests share something that stopped me in my tracks. Former NFL lineman Ed McGlasson talked about the importance of the father's blessing and how prophetic it can be. He shared about the countless men and women who never received a blessing from their parents and how this important missing piece impacted their lives in various ways. Maybe you didn't receive a father's blessing. Open your hands today. Your Father God has a blessing just for you. You are His beloved one, and He wants to make something beautiful of your life.

Maybe, right now, you're alone in marriage, or single, even. You're without a man to stand by your side and offer your children the blessing God has for them. This does not mean that your kids are some of the "have-nots." Painful as it is not to have a godly, loving husband at your side, God is still available to *you* and to work through you. Don't let your circumstances hinder your faith. Let them propel you to an even stronger belief that God is one your side. The best faith stories come out of impossible odds. God is with you. He has a blessing for you and your children.

Often at conferences Ed steps in and prays a blessing over many who have never received a godly blessing from their parents. People desperately want to know the Father's love and the specific inheritance they have in Him. Rarely is there a dry eye in the room when he finishes praying for those in need.

One day while ministering in a prison, Ed asked the inmates, "How many of your fathers or mothers told you that you'd end up in a place like this?" Guess how many prisoners raised their hands? Every single one of them.[3]

One day when my kids were about three, five, and seven, I sat on a lawn chair and watched them play kick ball in the backyard with some neighborhood boys. I battled extreme fatigue from the Lyme disease, and even the smallest tasks seemed an effort to me. Even so, it was a beautiful day to sit and rest and observe these little men work out their game issues. It was fun for me to watch their intensity of purpose and passion.

Jake kicked the ball, and it sailed to the edge of the yard. He rounded first base and landed on second. Next, it was their friend Johnny's turn. Though sports wasn't his thing, he was excited to be a part of the game. Just when the ball came rolling his way, his mother walked to the edge of the yard and started yelling at him, "Johnny, you left a mess in the house *again!* You are such a bad, bad boy! You never listen!"

Before any of us could say anything, Jake raised his hand and said, "Uh, Mrs. Olson, Johnny's not a bad boy. He's a good boy. He just made a bad choice." At that, she turned around in a huff and stormed off.

The thing was, Johnny didn't listen. He made loads of bad choices and was extremely frustrating to deal with. I felt sorry for his mom because he was a handful to manage. But I felt more sorry for him. How many of his exasperating habits were born out of his mother's constant yelling and berating?

To provide a balance here—and I've mentioned this throughout the book—we are going to blow it from time to time. We are going to say things we don't mean or wish we didn't feel. But our words are powerful. They go out from our mouths and into our children's souls. And if not dealt with, those negative words will embed themselves in our children's memories and become a part of their belief system. Our kids are like blank canvases. We paint a picture of who they are with the words we speak to them.

To reference Gary Smalley's insights once again: "We must not let our kids walk away with a closed spirit." When we blow it, we need to fix it.

Whenever we have authority or power over someone—be it a child, an employee, or even someone in a church setting—we have the opportunity to wield that power to our advantage. Without a holy fear of God, we as parents, leaders, and bosses can walk all over people and use them to our advantage.

> we are going to **BLOW IT** from time to time. We are going to say things we don't mean or **WISH WE DIDN'T FEEL.** But our words are **POWERFUL.** They go out from our mouths and into our children's **SOULS.**

Any time we have power over someone, we have the opportunity to misuse that power.

How many times have you been out and about and have seen a mom or dad shamelessly scream at their child in public, "Walk faster, you idiot!" Or "Shut up and get in the car!" And what is the child's response? He walks faster. She shuts up and gets in the car. I've seen a mom spout to her daughter, "Go get me a soda." And the child complies.

When parents are rude, short-tempered, or reactionary, they can get a child to quickly comply with their demands. *For a while.* But every time parents (or a leader) misuse their God-given authority, they drain some of the equity from their influence.

In other words, reactionary parents may get an immediate, desired result by getting "big" and bullying the child into submission, but in the long run they will lose the power of their impact over that child. When those same parents try to get their children to do the right thing, their words will seem disingenuous or hypocritical at best. And in due season, the child will grow into an angry teenager whose disillusionment will be directly related to the parents' misuse of authority and the absence of their blessing.

Another way to lose the equity of your influence is to be apathetic or uninvolved. If we're not constantly engaged, proactively so, we will diminish the influence we have in our children's lives. If it seems we don't have any strong opinions one way or another with regard to our child's life and his or her dreams and aspirations, then our opinions won't carry much weight when it really counts.

The same applies to leaders in every facet of life. The best leaders and the best parents are those who have a humble fear of God and a deep concern for those they lead. They know that ultimately they are accountable to the Lord for the way they wield their authority. And they hold that role in the highest regard. They steward the honor and respect their role deserves. And they never take advantage of their position, which, incidentally, strengthens their stance to lead and guide those for whom they are responsible.

The reason it's important to look at the misuse of authority is because it helps us to understand what a powerful position God has entrusted to us as parents of our children. Our role in our child's life is of supreme importance. We have power over our kids for a few short years. What will we do with those formative years? Will we bless or will we curse? Will we build equity into our influence and use that influence to set our children up for success? Or will we drain the authority God has entrusted to us by misusing our privileged authority? Will we speak life to them, or will our words and choices drain life from them?

> we have power over our kids for a **FEW SHORT YEARS.** What will we do with those **FORMATIVE** years? Will we **BLESS** or will we **CURSE?**

This day I call heaven and earth as witnesses against you that I have set before you life and death, blessings and curses. Now choose life, so that you and your children may live and that you may love the Lord your God, listen to his voice, and hold fast to him. (Deuteronomy 30:19–20)

Giving a blessing is easy. It's supremely important. Our children need to know who they are to us. They need to know how God sees them. It's up to us to tell them how valuable they are. They must learn about what they possess in Christ from us. All of these things can be communicated in a simple blessing. Or in one of many blessings: "Do you know how honored I am to be your mom? God had such a great idea when He created you! He has a great plan for your life. I believe you are going to reach lots of people for Christ."

Or, "You have so much compassion; I believe God is going to use you to minister to the sick and the hurting."

Or, "You are so organized; I believe God is going to use you to accomplish great things for an important business or ministry!"

I love the idea of everyday blessings. In an interview with *Christianity Today*, former NFL pro Bill Glass said this:

I found my kids love to be hugged and kissed. I grab my little girl by her ears and look into her eyes and say, "I love you, I bless you, I think you're absolutely terrific." That's easy with her because she's little and dainty. But I've got two boys, 280 and 290 pounds. One played pro ball, and both played college ball. They're 6'6", bench press 500 pounds, and are bigger than I am, but I grabbed that eldest son of mine recently and said, "I love, I bless you, I think you're terrific, and I'm so glad you're mine." His shoulders began to shake and his eyes filled with tears and he said, "Dad, I really needed that."

It's got to be said out loud. It's got to be stated. It's not like the lawyer that's getting a divorce and the judge says, "How often did you tell your wife you loved her?" and he replies, "I told her the day I married her and then never told her differently."

The blessing is also unconditional and continuous. If it's conditional, it's not love; it's a negotiation.[4]

Bill Glass's article specifically addressed the father's blessing. Whole books have been written on this very topic. The importance of the father's role in his children's lives cannot be overstated. Even so, it is important and effective for both Mom and Dad to bless their children. On a regular basis.

Remind them who they are. Tell them what they mean to you. Seek God for insights into their character and their God-given destiny. When the Lord created your beautiful child, He had a specific calling in mind for him or her. Right now He is working behind the scenes, engineering circumstances, and working on divine appointments for your child because their life is *that* important to Him! As far as God is concerned, your child is an absolute masterpiece. A treasure to be treasured. A gift to be nurtured. And a life bursting with potential.

> as far as God is concerned, YOUR CHILD is an absolute MASTERPIECE. And a life bursting with POTENTIAL.

For we are God's workmanship, created in Christ Jesus to do good works, which God prepared in advance for us to do. (Ephesians 2:10)

As we lean in and listen to the Father's insights for our child, we then become a messenger of His grace and a catalyst of His love. As we listen to Him, may we speak to our children. May we breathe life into their dreams. May we inspire courage to overcome their fears. And may we cooperate with God's refining work in their lives.

This kind of insight and involvement begs *us* for a vested walk of faith and an otherworldly kind of perspective. But isn't that what this world needs? Tomorrow's leaders are today's children. May we bless our children that they may grow up to fulfill the mighty calling on their lives.

personal application:

- If you never received a blessing from your parents, ask God for one. Ask Him to show you a trusted, godly person who can pray a blessing over you.

- Remind yourself daily that YOU are the object of God's great affection. Thank Him regularly for the great call on your life.

- Bless yourself and others. God calls us to speak to others that we may build them up, strengthen, and encourage them. May we be conduits of the Father's blessing!

parental application:

- Put your child's face in your hands today, look him or her in the eyes, and communicate your love, favor, and blessing.

- Ask God for divine insight into your child's calling. Set aside special family times and offer a more specific blessing to each child.

- During difficult times of discipline, recast a godly vision to your child. Remind him or her how valuable and called he or she is.

Precious Father,

I receive the blessing You have for me. Show me more clearly how You feel about me! Help me to believe You and live out all of the great things You planned before I was ever born. Take me by the hand now and use me as a catalyst of blessing for my children. Speak to my heart, show me Your way, and help me to clearly convey Your heart to them. You are good and wonderful and true. Help me to be a reliable messenger. Amen.

look for the victory

GOD IS WITH YOU

Give thanks to the Lord, call on his name; make known among the nations what he has done. Look to the Lord and his strength; seek his face always. Remember the wonders he has done, his miracles, and the judgments he pronounced. **(PSALM 105:1, 4–5)**

"Nothing brings God greater joy than when one of His children defies the odds."[1]

— MARK BATTERSON

---

growing up in Luke's shadow was not an easy thing to do, especially for a meek and mild child like Jordan. Since he was particularly accommodating, Jordan's desires were easy to miss. And since he was so very generous, it was easy to take advantage of him. Jordan was a man of few words. If someone else dominated the conversation, Jordan was happy to stay quiet. Jordan would have been an easy one to neglect because he didn't ask for much. God gave us Jordan right in the midst of the most trying times in our lives. Like a ray of sunshine on a cold, winter day, Jordan came into the world to bless us all.

More than anything else, kindness and gentleness marked Jordan's life. Even so, both Kevin and I noticed that intermingled with his sweetness, Jordan possessed a certain measure of fear and insecurity. I knew I needed to address these issues with Jordan, but I needed to talk with God about them first.

Finally, one day I sat down with my little boy and said, "Jordan, if you're shy in that you have less to say, that's okay. But if you're shy because you think *you* are less-than, well, that's *not* okay. We will not let you grow up believing a lie about yourself! You are something special to God! Do you know that His heart beats out of His chest when He looks at you? If you are in a room where everyone likes the color red, and you're the only one who likes the color blue, that's okay! Blue is great for you! You are no better than anyone else, but you are not less-than either! You have opinions and insights that matter, and God has given you some things to say. It's so important for you to understand your worth in Christ because it will affect every decision you make. If you want to be the person God intended you to be, and if you want to do all of the great things He has planned for you to do, you must dare to believe that you are *everything* to Jesus. And to us. Because you are!"

This was one of many conversations we had with Jordan about his value in Christ. Little by little, one step at a time, we saw him grow into a grateful, confident kid. He was happy to be generous when it suited him, but he stopped thinking he had to buy his way out of an identity hole. He was still flexible with plans, movies, and backyard games, but he stepped up and offered his opinion when it really mattered to him. It's like the true parts of him were preserved while the un-true parts of him were weeded out.

When he reached his middle school years, he was a different boy altogether. You couldn't make that kid feel insecure. From the top of his head to the tips of his toes, Jordan knew who he was. And he developed a wacky sense of humor.

Jordan owned a life-size stuffed gorilla that he had won at a carnival. One day I found him out in the garage emptying all of the stuffing into the garbage. "What are you doing, Jordan?" I asked. Flashing me a dimpled smile, he said, "Tomorrow is 'dress-like-your-twin' day."

Feeling a bit confused, I tilted my head, pointed to the furry mass in his hand, and asked, "And what does this unstuffed gorilla have to do with you and your supposed twin?" Still smiling he said, "Once I get all of this stuffing into the garbage, I'm going to wear this gorilla suit to school. I'll have a mirror with me so I can be my own twin."

The next morning, my seventh grade gorilla rode his bike to school. I watched Jordan ride away wearing his gorilla suit, with his backpack on his back and the ape head in one hand. Throughout the day I wondered what people were saying to him. I chuckled at the thought of him walking down the hall at school wearing that ridiculous ape costume.

Silly as it sounds, that day is marked in my memory as a day that I put a victory flag in the ground for my son.

Though it happened over time, the insecure and self-aware little boy who didn't think his opinion mattered was gone. Jordan was becoming his own man. He was learning to find his place in our family and in his world. Oh, he was more than just a goofy adolescent boy who was willing to wear a stuffed animal to school. Jordan defied the enemy's plan for him.

The devil would have loved for Jordan to grow into a wallflower, or an unassertive employee, or a spineless husband. Today Jordan, though still gentle, is very strong. He takes initiative when he needs to. He doesn't waver in the wind, and it doesn't even occur to him to doubt his value. He knows his opinion matters and that God has given him some things to say. As a young adult, he is now stepping into the plans God has for him. Though he is not yet all he will be (and neither am I), he's not *at all* who he used to be. And that's a victory worth celebrating.

> God won't LEAD US into any battle we can't WIN. Which means, EVERY BATTLE we face is a WINNABLE one.

❈ ❈ ❈

Every time we win a victory, we change the course of our lives and of those we are appointed to touch. The enemy has his plans and the Lord has His. Day and night the battle rages overhead for our souls, our perspectives, our choices, and our thoughts. But the Bible says that *overwhelming victory* is ours in Christ Jesus (see Romans 8:37). God won't lead us into any battle we can't win. Which means, every battle we face is a winnable one.

Our job as parents is to discern the battlegrounds where the enemy intends to wage war against our children. Is it fear? Insecurity? Selfishness? Rebellion? The devil is evil through and through.

He sees the potential in our children and would love nothing more than to wrap them up in self-sins and earthbound struggles, and thus alter the whole course of their lives.

The thief comes only to steal and kill and destroy; I have come that they may have life, and have it to the full. (John 10:10)

The devil intended for Moses to be a stuttering, stammering, self-aware man. But God intended for Moses to be a freedom fighter and to lead a nation of people out of captivity. The devil intended for Jonah to be a lily-livered scaredy-cat, but God had plans for Jonah to deliver a life-and-death message to the people of Nineveh. The devil worked hard to convince Joseph that he belonged at the bottom of a pit or in a dungy prison, but in the end, God's plan prevailed, and Joseph ruled from a palace.

The enemy intended for Harriet Tubman to live and die as a slave, but God's plan for her to heroically lead hundreds of other slaves to freedom changed history. The enemy wanted Corrie ten Boom to die in the concentration camp like some of her family members. But God had plans for Corrie to live out of a suitcase and tell the whole world about Jesus.

A Bible professor once shared this very interesting insight with me, "When I was a teen, I had almost an insatiable craving to do drugs, which, as you know, ruins the brain. God gave me a gift of intelligence and a high capacity for learning. Do you suppose the enemy saw my learning potential and sought to destroy and diminish the very gift God gave to me?" Her comment got me thinking about my own life. When I was a young girl and some teenage boys pinned me down, I couldn't scream. I opened my mouth but no sound came out. For the many years that followed, I had recurring dreams of being chased and attacked, but in my dream I had no voice to yell for help.

To make matters worse, those childhood experiences made me painfully insecure. In spite of the fact that I had loving parents, I still couldn't comprehend God's love. Even though I was a cheerleader and a gymnast in high school and somewhat associated with the popular crowd, I really wasn't a legitimate member of the group. I had no sense of self and constantly said the wrong thing at the wrong time. The enemy's loud and clear message to me was this: *You have no voice. You don't matter! Your voice doesn't matter. You always mess up what you're trying to say anyway!*

Jump ahead thirty years. I'm now an author, a speaker, and an occasional radio host for a live talk show. At my events I pray with women in desperate pain, and I have to be in tune with the Holy Spirit so that my words bring healing and encouragement and nothing less. When I'm live on the air and people call in and share about betrayal, infidelity, brokenness, or sickness, I have to be able to think on my feet and handle their situations with the utmost of care.

Many times over the past years I've had women say these words to me: "You ministered deeply to me today. I'm amazed at how you always say the right thing at the right time." I cannot tell you how *much* those words reinforce God's victory in my life. When I was an insecure, self-aware young teen, I never could have imagined that my weakness would someday—by the grace of God—become a strength that He could use to help others in their time of need.

When they are especially young, our kids may not notice or even care about the budding weaknesses within them. But given time to sprout, those very things will trip them up in their adolescent and teen years. Ideally, with God's help, we will discern those vulnerabilities while our kids are still young when we can easily correct and redirect them. It's better and easier to uproot little sprouts of fear, anger, worry, or insecurity before they have a chance to send their roots down into the soil of our children's character.

Even so, it's important to note that sometimes even our best intentions fall short. We may do everything we know to do and our kids may still battle some major weaknesses and vulnerabilities. Life is hard sometimes. Friends are cruel sometimes. Emotions overtake us sometimes. And our kids have a lot to sort through with all of the mixed messages coming their way.

When our children are tormented or tripped up by their weaknesses, we need to help them *imagine* what victory looks like. We need to give them tools to achieve that victory. Tools such as faith, exposure to God's Word, identity with other believers (by getting them to church and youth group functions), and our own stories of triumph and answered prayer. Out of our life experiences, Jesus has given us a brush and a palette to paint a picture for our children. May our life's

> it's **BETTER** and easier to uproot little sprouts of **FEAR, ANGER, WORRY,** or **INSECURITY** before they have a chance to send their **ROOTS** down into the soil of **OUR CHILDREN'S** character.

canvas portray Jesus' words: "Everything is possible if you believe" (see Mark 9:23).

In order to give our children the best possible chance at success, we need to look at their weaknesses and at the ways the enemy comes at them, and then take those things to God in prayer. We can pray a prayer something like this: *Lord, God, Your Word tells me that the enemy comes to steal, kill, and destroy everything that's good in our lives. But You come that we might have life abundantly. You know how my child is struggling. You know the lies the devil is sending her way. Show me what the opposite blessing looks like! Since the devil is the father of lies, I know he is lying to my child. You are the author of truth. What's the truth in this situation? What are You up to in my child's life? What is Your plan for her life? Help me to convey a victory plan for my precious child. Help us to defy the devil's plan and to fulfill Your highest and best will for us! Amen.*

God is more than happy to answer those kinds of prayers. He is all about victory! In fact, the Christian walk of faith calls us to battles and conquests, to go from one victory to another. We are not meant to simply respond to life as it comes at us. We are called by God to go after everything Christ Jesus has offered us. The enemy will oppose us. Trials will confront us. Fear will threaten us. But God calls us onward, one step at a time, from strength to strength and victory to victory. Pressing on to be all God intended us to be.

You give me your shield of victory, and your right hand sustains me; you stoop down to make me great. (Psalm 18:35)

In his wonderful book *In a Pit with a Lion on a Snowy Day*, author Mark Batterson tells about a time when his family took a trip to Nashville, Tennessee. They were all excited to stay at a hotel with a pool and enjoy some fun family time in the water. Once they got down to the pool, four-year-old Josiah decided he didn't want anything to do with the water. His reason? "I don't want to sink." This made no sense because Josiah always loved the water and had no fear when it came to jumping into the water with his dad.

Suddenly Mark had a flashback and remembered the last time they were in a pool. Little Josiah slipped in the shallow end and took a gulp of water. That memory changed Josiah's reference point. This was a new day. With outstretched arms, Josiah's dad invited him to jump. Even though his dad was right there with him, promising to catch him, Josiah's fears seemed bigger still. Read the author's insight into this situation:

I think most of us are shaped, for better or for worse, by a handful of experiences. Those defining experiences can plant a seed of confidence or a seed of doubt, a seed of hope or a seed of helplessness, a seed of faith or a seed of fear. In this instance, Josiah's sinking experience planted a seed of fear. And it is my job as a parent to pull that emotional weed so Josiah doesn't let an irrational fear of hotel pools take root in this mind. One of my sacred duties as a parent is to help my children unlearn their fears. That is why I took Josiah into the pool against his will. I tried not to traumatize him. And his screaming made me feel like a terrible parent. But I took him into the pool because it is my responsibility as a parent to help my kids face their fears. I knew fear wouldn't go away if he didn't learn to face it. And I knew he would forfeit so much fun if I didn't help him be brave.[2]

Our heavenly Father stands with outstretched arms and beckons us to jump! He doesn't want us bound by past fears or bad experiences. He doesn't want us to miss out on all of the fun. He wants us to join Him on a great adventure.

> **God ISN'T INTERESTED in making our lives COMFORTABLE. He wants to make our lives COUNT.**

Look back over the course of your own life and notice the victories. Finish this sentence as many times as you can: *I once was . . . and now I'm . . .*

Celebrate what God has done in your own life. Let those victories fuel you to fight for your child's utmost freedom. Pay close attention to consistent patterns of weakness and insecurity within your children. Not so that you can emphasize those things above his or her strengths, but so that you can help him or her uproot those weeds that threaten to choke out life and health.

Want a grateful child? Help him take on the giants in his land! Help her to have a face-off with her fears. As we stand with our children and dare to say, "Though the enemy would love to defeat you here, God wants to promote you here! Stand strong. Believe the truth. And let's see what God will do!" It takes some energy and some grit to go after the land that God has promised to our children, and the enemy won't give it up without a fight.

In fact, it's much more convenient to hide from the battle than it is to run to it. It's much *easier* to make our children comfortable or to coddle their weaknesses than it is to help them uproot a weed. But God isn't interested in making our lives comfortable. He wants to make our lives count. He wants us to live significant lives. And we want the same for our kids, wouldn't you say?

From the Lord comes deliverance. May your blessing be on your people. (Psalm 3:8)

Life on earth is a battle. Every single day the forces of evil and good clash and collide. Every single day we have the choice between blessing and curses, between life and death. We wouldn't need victory if we weren't engaged in a battle. But God's Word promises that victory belongs to those who belong to Him. One of my favorite authors, Catherine Marshall, had this to say about the battles we face:

"The Bible story of the conflict between good and evil is not downbeat at all, but upbeat; it is the story of the total defeat of the evil because of the absolute power of Christ."[3]

Look for victory in the life of your family. Picture it. Imagine someday sitting at the dinner table with your teen and saying, "Isn't it amazing what God has done in your life? You once were filled with fear and now you are going on a mission trip! May you never let the devil bully you out of the promised places God has for you!"

Now imagine walking with your adult child as she pushes her

baby's stroller. You turn to her and say, "Look at what God has done in your life! You were painfully shy as a child and now you and your husband have a ministry to young people. You are bearing fruit and gaining strength in the *very* area where you were once weak. May this victory fuel you to take hold of everything God has for you!"

You've won victories that you probably haven't even stopped to notice. You may be engaged in a battle right now, but have lost sight of what's available to you in Christ Jesus. You may be able to look at your child and see areas of vulnerability that the enemy would love to leverage to his advantage.

Today is a good day to pause and consider the victories you've won. Notice the ways that you are stronger today than you were last year. Embrace the idea that you are wiser and more seasoned as a parent than you once were. God is doing good things in you! Put a victory flag in the ground!

Today is a good day to renew your resolve to win the battles that are before you. The Bible is chock-full of promises that match your situation perfectly. You have everything you need and then some to be victorious in battle. Don't grow weary. Don't move away from courage (or be *dis*-couraged). Stand strong in the Lord. Deliverance will come.

Today is a great day to grab your child by the hand, walk with her, and recount the ways God altered the course of your life. At an age appropriate level point out how things could have gone if God would not have intervened. Talk about your victory flag moments. Impart faith along with an understanding that battling for victory is a necessary part of the Christian life. And the great news is this: we are more than conquerors through Christ Jesus.

The living, the living—they praise you, as I am doing today; fathers tell their children about your faithfulness. (Isaiah 38:19)

personal application:

- Write down some of your most significant personal victories. Continue to thank God for those outcomes. This will build your faith.

- (Forgive the personal plug here, but) read my book *Embracing Your Freedom*. It will help you to walk in the freedom God intended for you.

- In what way do you feel limited or tied up right now? Consider that to be your "next place of promise." Ask God to help you secure freedom and victory. Press on and don't give up!

parental application:

- Ask the Lord to help you discern the areas of vulnerability in your child's life. Start praying for opportunities to uproot, redirect, teach, and impart fresh seeds into his or her life.

- Notice the victories already won in your child's life. Talk about this with your child. Be amazed together at how far they've come. This will be a great motivator for him or her.

- Continually ask God to give you a vision for your child's life so that you can cooperate with Him in its fulfillment. Ask the Lord to give your child a heart for his or her call at a very young age so they will make choices to line up with that wonderful call.

Precious Lord,

Thank You for winning the ultimate victory for me! Because You went to the cross, I can walk in freedom. Help me to embrace the life You paid such a high price for. Let me not be satisfied in captivity. I want it all, Lord! Help me too to discern the areas in my kids that You what to shore up, fortify, and protect. I want to work with You to raise these precious little lambs. Give me eyes to see, ears to hear, and a brave heart to do Your will. Amen.

give grace

GOD DOES

Therefore, there is now no condemnation for those who are in Christ Jesus. (**ROMANS 8:1**)

"Driven not by our beauty but by his promise, he calls us to himself and invites us to take a permanent place at his table. Though we often limp more than we walk, we take our place next to the other sinners-made-saints and we share in God's glory."[1]

—MAX LUCADO

The other morning I woke up with a little knot in my stomach. I rolled over in bed, stared out the window, and prayed, "What's this about, Lord?" Nothing came to me, so I sat up in bed, walked over to the window, and waited for the sun to peek through the trees. I think sunrises and early mornings are some of God's best ideas. Even so, my heart was unsettled, and I needed to figure out why.

I grabbed my cup of chai tea, my Bible, my journal, and a few other quiet time necessities and I headed outside to my deck swing. My happy place. I propped up my iPhone, hit play on my devotional song play list, hugged my warm cup of chai, and inhaled the fresh morning air.

As I listened to the words of a particular song, my thoughts roamed back to the day before. I had run into an old friend-acquaintance. We talked back and forth and caught up on our lives. I was about to share something about my life when the Holy Spirit whispered, "Not safe. Don't share that." I held my peace and listened to my friend's updates. But somewhere later on in the conversation, I went ahead and shared a part of my heart that God specifically had told me not to! She probably didn't notice, but I was instantly convicted that I blatantly disobeyed a very clear directive from the Lord.

We wrapped up our conversation, and I prayed the whole way home. Now this may sound like a little thing to some of you, and a big-fat-act-of-disobedience to others, but either way, I knew better. I apologized to God, and I strongly sensed His love and forgiveness. And more than anything, I knew He was just trying to protect me.

So there I sat, hugging my cup of tea, completely wowed by the sunrise, when I realized that the fist in my gut was condemnation. The enemy had accused me all night long for being disobedient and ignorant. I woke up feeling bogged down by guilt, which cost me a whole night's sleep.

That's the enemy's MO, you know; he seduces us, and then accuses us for being such a dope for falling into his trap. Condemnation throws us down, weighs us down, and intends to keep us down . . . as long as we are willing to entertain its wretched presence.

But then there's God.

His morning mercies are a priceless gift to us. He forgives, restores, and renews us in a moment's time. He uses us on Monday knowing we're going to blow it on Tuesday. His Holy Spirit comforts and corrects us. He directs us and helps us distinguish truth from the lie. He brings conviction when we stray and correction when we need it.

Like the morning sunrise, the conviction of the Holy Spirit compels us to look up to Jesus, to stand up on His promises, and to rise up from the ash heap of our self-sins and be done with lesser things! Romans 8:1 is a blessed promise for us: "Therefore, there is now NO condemnation for those who are in Christ Jesus!"

Read this wonderful passage from *The Message* paraphrase:

> *With the arrival of Jesus, the Messiah, that fateful dilemma is resolved. Those who enter into Christ's being-here-for-us no longer have to live under a continuous, low-lying black cloud. A new power is in operation. The Spirit of life in Christ, like a strong wind, has magnificently cleared the air.* (Romans 8:1–2)

> The Holy Spirit **CALLS US** *up* when we sin. The devil, on the other hand, knocks **US DOWN.**

As parents, we love our children. We cherish them. The very fact that you are reading this book is a testament of your commitment to your little lambs and to their character. When we as Christ-followers sincerely try to do the right thing and we fail, we become prime targets for condemnation, self-loathing, self-criticism, and guilt. The Holy Spirit calls us *up* when we sin.

The devil, on the other hand, knocks us *down*. How do we reconcile our humanity with God's love? How do we turn a deaf ear to the accuser of our souls and yet be humble enough to admit it when we're wrong?

We embrace God's grace. For ourselves. And for our children. We desperately need Jesus. We are a work in progress. And so are they. Though we absolutely must raise our kids at a much higher standard than what society calls normal, we are going to fall short in more ways than one. At some point, we need to let go of our perfectionist ideas, do our divine best, and then rest on the goodness and the grace of almighty God. He more than makes up for the countless ways we are deficient.

I guess that's what makes grace so amazing to me. God lavishes love and forgiveness on us in almost a wasteful way. His gift seems beyond extravagant because we miss so much of His loving intent toward us. Some of it spills on us, and some of it falls by the wayside because we cannot imagine or comprehend the depth of our need or the height of His love. But He loves us still. He forgives us deeply though we only understand the surface of our sin. Just yesterday I wrote these words in my journal:

O Precious Lord,
I don't know how to thank You for a gift I cannot comprehend.
My mind cannot grasp the height of Your love, or the depth of
my offense.
But You gave me salvation anyway.
When I see Your face, I know I'll love fully, even as I'm fully
loved. I'll know fully, even as I'm fully known.

And for a brief second, I'll understand the depth of my sin and its far-reaching effects.

I'll know that Your forgiveness covered ground I didn't even know existed.

But while I was yet a sinner, You forgave me.
You loved me in spite of myself.
O, Jesus, You are precious to me.
I love that You love me. I love You too. Amen.

❀ ❀ ❀

We are imperfect parents led by a most perfect God. May He give us great discernment to quickly distinguish between conviction over our sin and condemnation over our mistakes! One protects the freedom we enjoy in Christ, and the other tosses us into prison. And it's *for freedom* that Christ has set us free!

Looking back over the years, now that my kids are grown, I can see traces of my humanity all over my kids' lives. While I did some things right, I also did plenty of things wrong. We had lots of great intentions and a few good ideas, but at the end of the day, my husband and I are still human. We were selfish or distracted on occasion and completely ignorant at times. But we loved our sons more than life. More than anything, we wanted to raise them to know Jesus, to respect authority, and to be humble souls. And thanks be to God— they are all of those things.

Still, as we watch them walk on their sometimes-wobbly adult legs, we can spot ways that could have better prepared them for this next stage of life. Their struggles thoroughly confront me. For a while there, I battled condemnation over the thought of my shortcomings, but then Jesus reminded me that because of what He did for me, there is absolutely *no* room for condemnation in my life. So I settled into a place of grace. I did my best as their mom, and now I leave the rest with God. My main role in my sons' lives is now one of love and support (and earnest prayerful intercession behind the scenes).

More and more lately, I meet up with moms who approach the empty nest stage feeling burdened by regret and condemnation. Swirling through their thoughts are things like: *I shouldn't have ridden him so hard. Or, I should have followed through with discipline more often. Or, I was way too easy on her, and now she can't do anything for herself. Or, I wish I would have challenged his strong will on a more consistent basis. Or, I shouldn't have given her emotions such free rein. Or, I completely spoiled her, and now, as a young adult, all she thinks of is herself!*

Now the fact is, there are some serious consequences to going soft on our kids and of not following through with discipline. Even our society pays a price for the ways we neglect to train our kids. It is my prayer that a revival of godly parenting would spring forth in our land! But still, how do we deal with the fact that we are going to get it wrong some days? What are we supposed to do with the idea that our missteps will directly affect our children's lives? This past year I received the following e-mail from a friend:

> it is my **PRAYER**
> that a revival of
> **GODLY PARENTING**
> would spring forth
> in our **LAND.**

Do you think when I feel regret and like I could have done a better job as a mother that those feelings fit in to condemnation or is it conviction of something I did wrong? Is the difference about confession and accepting forgiveness, meaning once you have done that, then the guilt felt after that is condemnation? I think the tough part is that we are not perfect people, so we can't be perfect parents, so what do you do with the feelings that you have when you look back and see what you could have done differently? I have been pondering this, and then last night a friend said something interesting about having regrets as a mother and I thought *You too?* Wow. I sort of feel like it is Satan's way of getting me down because being a parent (to me) is one of the most important things I have ever done. I love being a mom so is this a way for Satan to "steal" joy from my life?!! Very interesting ponderings going on in my brain today! ☺

And here is a portion of my response to her:

Regarding your thoughts about guilt, condemnation, and conviction around raising our children, I'm learning that the enemy *loves* to throw this stuff our way when we transition into the empty nest season. He knows that our job is basically done (you know what I mean) and that we cannot go back and undo anything, do more of something, or do better at something. He loves to corner us and make us feel stuck.

As I've told you before, I have one son in Nashville, one about to get married, and Jordan, who is about to graduate. Now that they are learning to stand on their wobbly adult legs (it's like watching your baby learn how to walk all over again), I see several areas where I could have been stronger and more efficient as a mom. I went through the guilt and the feeling bad, until one day I realized those things weren't from God. He showed me some insights on how I could have done a better job. I asked for forgiveness for the ways I fell short. I asked Him to take my imperfect offering of motherhood (like the little boy's lunch that Jesus used) and multiply it to meet their need. Then I spoke with my boys and shared about those feelings. I said, "You know, I can

> **any unhealthy adult who keeps BLAMING HIS PARENTS for all of his own SHORTCOMINGS will never get anywhere in life.**

see now that I could have been stronger in this area with you. I'm sorry I wasn't. Still, I hope you will take the great start you've been given, and build upon it; just like your dad and I did with what we were given."

Any unhealthy adult who keeps blaming his parents for all of his own shortcomings will never get anywhere in life. At some point we—as adults who had imperfect parents—have to brush ourselves off, figure out where we are lacking, and get what we need from the Lord. *As do our children.* When I was able to have a heart-to-heart with my boys and then challenge them to take their gifts to the next level, it really took the burden off my shoulders.

So, all of that to say, after I did the work of repentance, I knew I needed to do the work of resisting the devil's attempts to steal my joy, as you said. Does that help? You are not alone! The devil overplays his hand every day of the week. And you are a wonderful mom. I can see the love for your boys shine on your countenance. They know you love them with every fiber in your being. That's a pretty big deal!

I pray that God fills you up with joy and freedom as you release those precious sons into adulthood. Okay, this was probably a longer answer than you were looking for. But I hope it helps.

Be blessed, my friend.

❁ ❁ ❁

May I speak frankly here? As a young mom, it's easy to approach parenting with a sense of idealism and even pride. You want to do things better than your parents did (and you should!), and you have your own ideas about how you want to raise your children (and you should!). But woven into the fabric of our ideals sometimes is a thread of pride and self-striving. If we're not careful, we'll embrace the mind-set that the older generations are not necessarily as wise as they actually are, and that we somehow have the corner on the truth about what it takes to raise exceptional children.

My advice is to be humble and cautious. Be open to the fact that some of your ideals will fly and others will fall flat. Understand that your parents may be wiser than you know, and that you just might be more ignorant than you realize. To the extent that you remain teachable and humble, especially during those dark nights of parenting, will determine just how easy it is for you to get back up again after you fall.

Jesus tried to issue Peter a similar caution. Peter was enthusiastic. I can imagine him raising his fist in the air and yelling, "Let's do this! Let's make disciples of men!" In His gentle-Jesus way, the Savior warned Simon Peter about the battles ahead:

"Simon, Simon, Satan has asked to sift you as wheat. But I have prayed for you, Simon, that your faith may not fail. And when you have turned back, strengthen your brothers". (Luke 22:31–32)

Jesus wasn't trying to diminish Peter's enthusiasm; He simply wanted Peter prepared for the road ahead. But Peter was still a bit full of himself. Read their next exchange:

But he replied, "Lord, I am ready to go with you to prison and to death." Jesus answered, "I tell you, Peter, before the rooster crows today, you will deny three times that you know me." (Luke 22:33–34)

In so many words, Jesus is saying, "Really? Really, Peter? You're ready to charge ahead full of self-confidence? You think you're ready to go all of the way with Me? In a little while, you're going to deny *even knowing Me*. But don't despair. I've made a way back for you. And when you finally realize that you can do nothing apart from Me, encourage others with what you've learned from Me. I love you no matter what."

Here's a translation of that scene for the modern-day mom who thinks she knows more than she does:

"Really? You're going to read all of the latest books and be the best parent this earth has every known? Well, the reality is that you'll have your good days when no one is looking, and you'll have days when everything unravels and you'll fail miserably. Sometimes when people look at you they may be surprised to find out that you are a woman of faith; but don't worry, because more is on God's shoulders than on yours. He has overcome the world. Do your best, and then leave the rest. At the end of the day, you are still God's greatest treasure, and everything is going to be okay."

The earth is full of God's unfailing love. His lavish grace is everywhere. When you blow it, give yourself some grace. When your kids act like the little humans that they are, correct them, teach them, forgive them, and then offer grace. Just as Christ has done for you. Trust me. Your kids will be eternally grateful to learn about God's grace from *you*.

We didn't come to Christ on the basis of our perfection. On the contrary, we came to Him on the basis of our need. We parent much the same way . . . not by our perfection, but by admitting our need. God knew what He was doing when He gave us our children. He had no illusions about us. Since that's true, may we do our best and then leave the rest in His hands. And, when it's time for our kids to move on, may their memories of grace—not of striving and straining, not of guilt and condemnation—be the thing that carries them through-out their lives. Give grace. God does.

Heaven is for sinners who face their sin; hell is for those who refuse to see. One of the ironic similarities between heaven and hell is that no one in either place thinks they got what they deserve.[2]

personal application:

• Spend a little time each morning admitting your need, confessing your weakness, and thanking God for His grace.

• Make allowances for the faults of others. Give grace even when you'd rather not.

• When you blow it, admit it; ask for forgiveness, and then refuse to let the enemy torment you with it again.

parental application:

• Spend some time with God; ask Him to show you ways in which you fall short as a parent. Ask Him for insight, direction, and forgiveness. And with His strength, do your best to make different choices.

• Take hold of every opportunity to teach your child about grace. Explain what it means to have a debt that you cannot pay. Read stories of extravagant forgiveness. Paint a big picture of grace for your child.

• When they are bothered with a sibling or a friend, help them to offer grace, just as they have received it. Write down their offenses on a piece of paper; then write their friend's or siblings offenses on a different piece of paper. Explain how either both of them go on the cross, or neither of them does. Teach grace.

give grace

Gracious Lord,

Thank You for Your lavish gift of grace. Help me to understand the vastness of this treasure. Increase my capacity to understand how deeply You love me and of what You've forgiven me. I never want to take Your grace for granted. And I never want to settle for a cheap, less-than version of what You intended for me. Your grace is sacred, holy ground. May I walk and live and breathe as though I fully understand this truth.

Amen.

be Like Christ

GOD LOVES YOU

Mostly what God does is love you. Keep company with him and learn a life of love. Observe how Christ loved us. His love was not cautious but extravagant. He didn't love in order to get something from us but to give everything of himself to us. Love like that. **(EPHESIANS 5:2 THE MESSAGE)**

"The task ahead of us is never as great
as the power behind us."[1]

—AUTHOR UNKNOWN

This has been a busy summer for me. Jordan graduated from high school, Luke got married, and I wrote two books in a row without more than a day's break in between. My emotions have surprised me this summer. I'm choked up one minute, anxious the next. Happy with glee another moment, and quiet with awe the next. So many transitions crammed into such a short time. I've felt in over my head in more ways than one.

A couple of weeks ago, my newly married son Luke stopped by for a visit. Just like old times, he sat on the kitchen counter, plucked a few chords on his guitar, and chatted with me while I washed dishes.

While strumming a nice chord progression, Luke said, "I wrote a new song today, Mom. Wanna hear it?" On that note, I pulled my sudsy hands out of the dishwater, dried them off, sat down at the kitchen table, and gave Luke my full attention. "This song is about how God sees us redemptively," he paused, "even though we are still very much works in progress. He sees us with a pure heart. The name of the song is 'The Angel in Me.'"

How completely ironic that as I'm getting ready to wrap up this book—one that mostly chronicles Luke's journey from feistiness to faith—that he would stop by and share a song about how God sees us on *His terms*. With a heart of pure, undefiled love.

One day when Luke was just a little boy, he challenged me in public, and a woman standing nearby said these words to me (right in front of him): "That kid is going to end up in jail someday." Shocked, I looked at her and then stooped down to Luke's level. I grabbed his chubby little shoulders and said, "Do you know that's not true, Luke? It's not true. God has some great plans for you!"

It wasn't true. God saw something different altogether. Here are some of the lyrics to Luke's new song:

The Angel in Me

You saw my heart before the world began
You called my name as I was crafted by your hand
I was created to be yours
To forever praise the name

be like Christ

Of the one who walks and the one who speaks
The one who heals and the one who sees

The angel inside of me

The greatness that I could be
Before the world began
I was created for your plan
And you gave me
Everything on earth
So I could echo the heavens and forever worship you

God sees the angel in me

© 2009 by Luke Larson

Since Luke's life served as much of the inspiration behind this book, I thought it fitting to close by sharing about one of his funnier moments. If you've ever heard me speak, no doubt you've heard this one before. But there's a twist. His story asks something from you as well.

Lukey was my chubby child. He had such a big belly that when he was a baby, he preferred the reclined position. Sitting upright seemed to cut off his air supply. One of his idiosyncrasies as a toddler was to strip down naked to go to the bathroom. I used to say to him, "Luke, that's the glory of being a boy! You don't have to get naked to go to the bathroom." Whenever I said anything that apparently didn't apply to him, he'd give me that deadpan stare as if to say, "Well, that's what *you* think."

One day while sitting on the toilet with the bathroom door wide open, he yelled down the hall in his questioning, demanding sort of way, "Mommm?!?" I stood up and yelled back, "Yes, Luke!" He continued, "Um, are you *sure* I'm supposed to ask Jesus into my heart?" I smiled and replied, "Yes, honey. I'm sure." But before I could go into my motherly explanation of why he needed Jesus, Luke spouted back, "Uh,' cuz I think I asked Him into my stomach. This thing is *huge!*"

Classic Lukester.

Something that I've learned in my years of following Christ is that He wants to be *in* every part of us. Funny as it sounds, may Christ be in our stomach! May our hunger for Him trump our earthly appetites and tendencies toward excess (see Psalm 63:1).

May Christ be in our head! May our thoughts default to praise instead of grumbling; faith instead of fear; trust instead of worry (see Philippians 4:8).

May Christ be in our eyes that we might see life, see ourselves, and see others just the way He does (see Psalm 105:4 and 2 Corinthians 5:16).

May Christ be in our mouth so that the first words to escape us are those of encouragement, truth, blessing, and perspective (see Proverbs 31:26 and Ephesians 4:29).

May Christ be in our ears that He may be a filter for what we allow in and what we keep out (see Mark 4:24).

May Christ be in our back that we may have a strong and sturdy backbone when it comes to righteousness, justice, and integrity (see Proverbs 31:9).

May Christ be in our hands that we may serve Him and love others with a healing touch (see Luke 10:9).

May Christ be in our knees that we will be quick to humble ourselves in prayer (see 1 Peter 5:6).

May Christ be in our feet that we may only go where He sends us (see Isaiah 52:7).

And may God's peace be our guide, and may we say no to every un-appointed task so that we may give Jesus our wholehearted yes (see Psalm 29:11).

We have this one life, this short time on earth to make our mark and to make life count. We have these children in our care for a blink of an eye. *Now* is the time to be engaged and fully present. *Now* is the time to seek divine insight into God's plan for their lives. *Now* is the time to rise up and be the parent that we might train our kids in the way they should go.

We are not alone. Not by a long shot. Yes, we have a seemingly impossible task before us, but we have Christ within us, and the heavens cheering for us. We can make a difference in this world! We can do every single thing God asks us to through Christ who gives us strength. Nothing is impossible for us! It doesn't matter that our society has fallen to an all-time low; in fact, this is the perfect time to rise up and be blessed. God's promises are as true as they've ever been. His call to live an otherworldly life is as real as it has ever been.

Will it be easy? Absolutely not! Will you cry yourself to sleep sometimes? That's a certainty. But would you want to be anywhere else? I hope not! God has ordained you and appointed you to bear life-giving fruit, and to leave an impact on this earth that lasts long after you're gone. Your children are part of that fruit. Invest in them.

Teach them about this living, breathing God we serve. It's not enough to bring them to church on Sundays and to get them to youth group on occasion. That won't be enough in the days ahead. Go after Jesus in your personal life. Live with breathless expectancy and marvel at everything He does. Because everything He does is worth noting.

Share what you learn with your children. Let the joy of your faith journey deeply impact your kids. Teach them not about rigid religion; teach them about love. And forgiveness. And faith. And hope. Help them to inherit the idea that, truly, nothing will be impossible for them if they will humble themselves before the Lord.

Cast a vision for what is possible for those who believe. Read stories of some of the spiritual greats who have gone before them. Tell your children that God wants them to change the world, because He does, you know. Never allow your walk with Jesus to become rote, or an ought-to, or a should-do.

Life with Jesus is unequivocally a *get-to*.

❁

❁

❁

What a journey this has been! As you walk forward from here, always remember that, first and foremost, *you are a woman of God*. Nurture and protect that relationship. Learn and live and grow in the knowledge of what it means to be linked in fellowship with your beautiful Creator. Your identity comes from Him. God has given you a husband to love and care for and children to raise, but more than these, *you are His.*

I pray that you are deeply inspired to walk closely with Jesus, to receive what He offers, that you might impart those gifts to your children. What an important job you have! *You are raising future world-changers.*

It's been my honor to walk this path with you. Be blessed, my friend.

For this reason I kneel before the Father, from whom his whole family in heaven and on earth derives its name. I pray that out of his glorious riches he may strengthen you with power through his Spirit in your inner being, so that Christ may dwell in your hearts through faith. And I pray that you, being rooted and established in love, may have power, together with all the saints, to grasp how wide and long and high and deep is the love of Christ, and to know this love that surpasses knowledge—that you may be filled to the measure of all the fullness of God. Now to him who is able to do immeasurably more than all we ask or imagine, according to his power that is at work within us, to him be glory in the church and in Christ Jesus throughout all generations, for ever and ever! Amen. (Ephesians 3:14–21)

NOTES

CHAPTER ONE: BE EXPECTANT

1. Elizabeth Barrett Browning quote from Heartlight.org (3/15/09).

2. Madeline L'Engle quote from Heartlight.org (7/6/06).

CHAPTER TWO: REFUSE WORRY

1. Oswald Chambers, quoted in *Draper's Book of Quotations for the Christian World* (Wheaton, Ill.: Tyndale, 1992), 657.

CHAPTER THREE: PRACTICE RESTRAINT

1. M. Scott Peck, quoted in *Draper's Book of Quotations for the Christian World*, ed. Edythe Draper (Wheaton, Ill.: Tyndale, 1992), 457.

CHAPTER FOUR: TAKE TIME TO PLAY

1. Martin Luther, quoted in *Draper's Book of Quotations for the Christian World*, ed. Edythe Draper (Wheaton, Ill.: Tyndale, 1992), 472.

2. Deborah Rather aka Arlene James emailed me these "family play" ideas on 6/5/06.

3. Hebrew translation of *delight* taken from the *NAS Old Testament Hebrew Lexicon* (Crosswalk.com); Strong's number: 6026.

4. Hebrew translation of *give* taken from the *NAS Old Testament Hebrew Lexicon* (Crosswalk.com); Strong's number: 5414.

5. Definition of *give* taken from the *NAS Old Testament Hebrew Lexicon* (Crosswalk.com); Strong's number: 5414.

CHAPTER FIVE: DEVELOP COMPASSION

1. Theodore Roosevelt quote taken from flip calendar, "Bless Your Heart: Samplers from the Heartland," compiled by Mary Bevis and Nini Sieck, 1987, February 1 reading.

2. Virginia Smith story first appeared as an article titled, "Lessons in Love" at http://www.cbn.com/spirituallife/Devotions/VirginiaSmith_christmaso5.aspx.

CHAPTER SIX: ASK FOR WISDOM

1. Eugene Peterson, *A Long Obedience in the Same Direction* (Downers Grove, Ill.: InterVarsity, 1980, 2000), 27.

2. Ron Hall and Denver Moore, *Same Kind of Different As Me* (Nashville: Thomas Nelson, 2008).

CHAPTER SEVEN: LIVE HUMBLY

1. St. Augustine of Hippo, quoted in *Draper's Book of Quotations for the Christian World*, ed. Edythe Draper (Wheaton, Ill.: Tyndale, 1992), 326.

2. John Fischer, *12 Steps for the Recovering Pharisee* (Minneapolis: Bethany 2000), 100–101.

3. Ibid., 102.

CHAPTER EIGHT: EMBRACE CONTENTMENT

1. G.K. Chesterton, quoted in *Draper's Book of Quotations for the Christian World*, ed. Edythe Draper (Wheaton, Ill.: Tyndale, 1992), 1825.

2. Linda Dillow, *Calm My Anxious Heart* (Colorado Springs: NavPress, 1998), 26.

3. Fred G. Gosman, *Spoiled Rotten* (New York: Villard Books, a division of Random House, Inc.,1990), 55, 124.

4. "Count Your Blessings," author unknown, source: www.iciworld.net.

CHAPTER NINE: TEACH FORGIVENESS

1. Martin Luther King Jr., quoted in *Draper's Book of Quotations for the Christian World*, ed. Edythe Draper (Wheaton, Ill.: Tyndale, 1992), 4084.

2. Joyce Meyer, *The Root of Rejection* (Tulsa, Okla.: Harrison House, 1994), 77.

CHAPTER TEN: LOOK DEEPER

1. Brennan Manning, *Ruthless Trust* (Tulsa, Okla.: Harper Collins, 2000), 19.

CHAPTER ELEVEN: PRAY BOLDLY

1. Andrew Murray, *Believing Prayer* (Minneapolis: Bethany House, 2004), 64.

2. A.W. Tozer, *The Pursuit of God: A 31 Day Experience*, compiled by Edythe Draper (Camp Hill, Pa.: Christian Publications, Inc., 1995), 46.

3. E.M. Bounds quote taken from flip calendar, "On My Knees," (Bloomington, Minn.: Garborg's, 2000), August 14 quote.

4. Bruce Wilkinson, *Beyond Jabez* (Sisters, Oreg.: Multnomah, 2005), 137.

CHAPTER TWELVE: SPEAK THE TRUTH

1. Joseph Joubert, quoted in *Draper's Book of Quotations for the Christian World*, ed. Edythe Draper (Wheaton, Ill.: Tyndale, 1992), 602.

CHAPTER THIRTEEN: GIVE A BLESSING

1. Bruce Wilkinson, *Beyond Jabez* (Sisters, Oreg.: Multnomah, 2005), 108.

2. The Sabbath idea came from Kery Wyatt Kent's book *Rest: Living in Sabbath Simplicity* (Grand Rapids, Mich.: Zondervan, 2009), 56.

3. Ed McGlasson quote from Don Moen's radio program, "Don Moen and Friends," August 16 broadcast, www.donmoen.com.

4. Bill Glass quote taken from the article "The Power of a Father's Blessing," *Christianity Today*, January 26, 2006 online edition, www.christianitytoday.com.

CHAPTER FOURTEEN: LOOK FOR THE VICTORY

1. Mark Batterson, *In a Pit with a Lion on a Snowy Day* (Sisters, Oreg.: Multnomah, 2006), 37.

2. Ibid. 47–48.

3. Catherine Marshall, *Something More* (New York: Inspirational Press, 1991), 130.

CHAPTER FIFTEEN: GIVE GRACE

1. Max Lucado, *In the Grip of Grace* (Dallas, Tex.: Word, 2006), 104.

2. John Fischer, *12 Steps for the Recovering Pharisee* (Minneapolis: Bethany, 2000), 58.

CHAPTER SIXTEEN: BE LIKE CHRIST

1. Unknown author quote from Heartlight.org (5/7/09).

ACKNOWLEDGMENTS

No book is the work of only one person. My deep and heartfelt thanks to all of you for your wonderful support and input!

A special thanks goes out to my sample readers who read each chapter as I wrote it and provided excellent feedback along the way:

Thank you, Daryl Jackson, Lisa Irwin, Mary Newberg, Carolyn Crust, Nancy Perry, Stephanie Johnson, Kathy Newberg, Larry and Karen Chapple, Jeannie Thyren, Ann Hinrichs, Judy Chesla, Bonnie Newberg, Liane Bloomquist, Cindy Larson, Leah Jackson, Gail Miller, Heidi Turner, Tanda Eidsvoog, Andie Munn, Tami Brown, Janet Nelson, Renee Volk, Renee Ihde, and Andrea Canniff. A special thanks goes out to Patty Larson. Bless you for your watchful eye! Thanks, everyone. I love you all!

Thanks to my intercessors. You know who you are. Bless you for holding up my arms when I'm tired, for standing in the gap when I need reinforcement, and for keeping heaven busy with your prayers! I so appreciate all of you!

Thank you, Ginny Smith and Arlene James, for your wonderful contributions to this book.

Thanks to my agent, Beth Jusino. I'm really going to miss you.

Bless you, my friend.

Thank you to my amazing and wonderful friends at Moody Publishers. I wouldn't want to be anywhere else but here! You've become a family to me, and I cherish every one of you. Special thanks to my publicist Janis Backing, to editor-in-chief, Steve Lyon, and to editors extraordinaire, Betsey Newenhuyse and Pam Pugh.

Thank you, Mom and Dad, for your wonderful presence in my life. Thanks too, Mom, for letting me read to you over the phone. I love you both so very much.

Bless you, Kevin, for your constant support in ministry and in life; and for your willingness to let this be a mom-to-mom book. Your role in our sons' lives has made all the difference in the world, and we all love you for it.

To my sweet sons: thank you for your willingness to share your life and your laundry with the rest of the world. You are truly grateful, humble guys. Your dad and I love and respect you more with each passing day.

And finally, to our heavenly Father ~ You are the best parent of all! Thank You for holding my hand, for whispering in my ear, for the promise of wisdom, and for Your constant love. You are everything to me.

Alone in Marriage

ISBN-13: 978-0-8024-5278-8

Often, when a woman ends up carrying the weight of the marriage (due to her husband's health, choices, workload, etc.), her tendency is to "get out or check out." She may consider her husband's distraction an opportunity to do her own thing. But is there a better way to walk through this season? Even thrive? Susie Larson stands in as an encouraging friend, walking with you, helping you to discern how anxiety and anger will slow you down; and how loneliness and disappointment can actually refine and bless you.

MOODY
PUBLISHERS
MoodyPublishers.com

UNCOMMON WOMAN

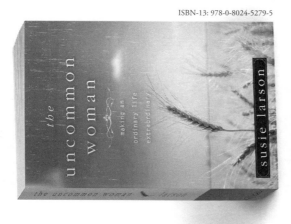

ISBN-13: 978-0-8024-5279-5

Imagine yourself in a pool of strong swimmers, all swimming clockwise. You, a Christian woman, are swimming counter-clockwise...counter-cultural, if you will. This book is for the woman who longs to rise up out of the stereotypical behavior of gossip, insecurity, pettiness, and small dreams. She has an unfulfilled desire to be someone who goes against the grain of the common for the sole purpose of living life with conviction. The woman who reads this book is ready to believe in her deep value, ready to accept her high calling, and ready to make a difference in a world in need of her influence.

MOODY
PUBLISHERS

MoodyPublishers.com

Embracing Your Freedom

ISBN-13: 978-0-8024-5280-1

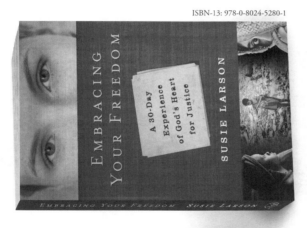

While our culture places great emphasis on comfort, security, control, and success, there are deeper rewards for those who take hold of God's promises and who thus reach out in the Name of Christ. Adventure, faith, miracles, and a deep knowledge of Jesus Christ: this is what Susie calls her readers to realize. Author/speaker Susie Larson makes her message accessible and doable. Her stories, scriptural devotionals, and study questions set the stage for a firsthand experience of God's heart for personal freedom, for the plight of the suffering, and for a conviction to get involved with His work among those in need.

MOODY
PUBLISHERS
MoodyPublishers.com